Table of Contents

Study Guide for the *Social Studies: Content Knowledge* Test
and the *Citizenship Education: Content Knowledge* Test

▶   ▶   ▶   ▶   ▶   ▶   ▶   ▶   ▶   ▶   ▶   ▶

Chapter 1
Introduction to *Social Studies: Content Knowledge and Citizenship Education: Content Knowledge* and Suggestions for Using this Study Guide 1

Chapter 2
Background Information on The Praxis Series Assessments 7

Chapter 3
An Overview of the Study Topics for the *Social Studies: Content Knowledge* Test and the *Citizenship Education: Content Knowledge* Test 13

Chapter 4
United States History: Study Topics 19

Chapter 5
World History: Study Topics 29

Chapter 6
Government and Civics: Study Topics 37

Chapter 7
Geography: Study Topics 41

Chapter 8
Economics: Study Topics 47

Chapter 9
Behavioral Sciences: Study Topics 55

Chapter 10
Don't Be Defeated by Multiple-Choice Questions 59

Chapter 11
Practice Questions 69

Chapter 12
Right Answers and Explanations for the Practice Questions 119

Chapter 13
Are You Ready? Last-Minute Tips 141

Appendix A
Study Plan Sheet 145

Appendix B
For More Information 149

Chapter 1

Introduction to *Social Studies: Content Knowledge* and *Citizenship Education: Content Knowledge* and Suggestions for Using this Study Guide

▶   ▶   ▶   ▶   ▶   ▶   ▶   ▶   ▶   ▶   ▶   ▶

Introduction to *Social Studies: Content Knowledge* and *Citizenship Education: Content Knowledge*

These tests are designed for prospective secondary social studies teachers. The tests are designed to reflect current standards for knowledge, skills, and abilities in social studies education. Educational Testing Service (ETS) works in collaboration with its client states, the National Council for Accreditation of Teacher Education (NCATE), and the National Council for the Social Studies (NCSS), along with teacher educators, higher education content specialists, and accomplished practicing teachers in the field of social studies to keep the test updated and representative of current standards.

The *Social Studies: Content Knowledge* test consists of 130 multiple-choice questions and covers six major areas. The *Citizenship Education: Content Knowledge* test consists of 115 multiple-choice questions and covers five major areas. It does not cover the behavioral sciences (sociology, anthropology, psychology).

Major Areas Covered by the Tests

Social Studies: Content Knowledge	*Citizenship Education: Content Knowledge*
◗ United States History	◗ United States History
◗ World History	◗ World History
◗ Government and Civics	◗ Government and Civics
◗ Geography	◗ Geography
◗ Economics	◗ Economics
◗ Behavioral Sciences (Sociology, Anthropology, Psychology)	—

The test questions are arranged in the test booklet by area. The questions are distributed across the major areas in the following proportions:

Major Areas	*Social Studies: Content Knowledge*	*Citizenship Education: Content Knowledge*
◗ United States History	22%	25%
◗ World History	22%	25%
◗ Government and Civics	16%	18%
◗ Geography	15%	16%
◗ Economics	15%	16%
◗ Behavioral Sciences (Sociology, Anthropology, Psychology)	10%	0%

Test takers have two hours to complete the test.

The test is not intended to assess teaching skills but rather to demonstrate the candidate's fundamental knowledge in the major areas of social studies.

Suggestions for Using the "Study Topics" Chapter of this Study Guide

This test is different from a final exam or other tests you may have taken in that it is comprehensive — that is, it covers material you may have learned in several courses during more than one year. It requires you to synthesize information you have learned from many sources and to understand the subject as a whole.

As a teacher, you will need a thorough understanding of the fundamental concepts in these six areas and the ways in which the various concepts fit together. You also need to understand typical misconceptions, because as a teacher you will need to apply your knowledge to situations in the classroom.

This test is very different from the SAT® or other assessments of your reading, writing, and mathematical skills. You may have heard it said that you can't study for the SAT—that is, you should have learned these skills throughout your school years, and you can't learn reading or reasoning skills shortly before you take the exam. The *Social Studies: Content Knowledge* test and *Citizenship Education: Content Knowledge* test assess a domain you *can* review for and can prepare to be tested on. Moreover, studying for your licensing exam is a great opportunity to reflect on your field and develop a deeper understanding of it before you begin to teach the subject matter to others.

We recommend the following approach for using the "Study Topics" chapters to prepare for the test.

Become familiar with the test content. Learn what will be tested in the test, covered in chapters 3 through 9.

Assess how well you know the content in each area. It is quite likely that you will need to study in most or all of the six areas. After you learn what the test contains, you should assess your knowledge in each area. How well do you know the material? In which areas do you need to learn more before you take the test?

Develop a study plan. Assess what you need to study and create a realistic plan for studying. You can develop your study plan in any way that works best for you. A "Study Plan" form is included in Appendix A at the end of the book as a possible way to structure your planning. Remember that this is a licensure test and covers a great deal of material. Plan to review carefully. You will need to allow time to find the books and other materials, time to read the material and take notes, and time to go over your notes.

Identify study materials. Most of the material covered by the test is contained in standard introductory textbooks in each of the major fields. If you do not own an introductory text in each area, you may want to borrow one or more from friends or from a library. You may also want to obtain a copy of your state's standards for social studies. (One way to find these standards quickly is to go to the Web site for your state's Department of Education.) The textbooks used in secondary classrooms may also prove useful to you, since they also present the material you need to know. Use standard school and college introductory textbooks and other reliable, professionally prepared materials. Don't rely heavily on information provided by friends or from searching the World Wide Web. Neither of these sources is as uniformly reliable as textbooks.

Work through your study plan. You may want to work alone, or you may find it more helpful to work with a group or with a mentor. Work through the topics and questions provided in chapters 3 through 9. Be able to define and discuss the topics in your own words rather than memorizing definitions from books. If you are working with a group or mentor, you can also try informal quizzes and questioning techniques.

Proceed to the practice questions. Once you have completed your review, you are ready to benefit from the "Practice Questions" portion of this guide.

Suggestions for Using the "Practice Questions" and "Right Answers and Explanations for the Practice Questions" Chapters

Read chapter 10 ("Don't Be Defeated by Multiple-Choice Questions"). This chapter will sharpen your skills in reading and answering questions. Succeeding on multiple-choice questions requires careful focus on the question, an eye for detail, and patient sifting of the answer choices.

Answer the practice questions in chapter 11. Make your own test-taking conditions as similar to actual testing conditions as you can. Work on the practice questions in a quiet place without distractions. Remember that the practice questions are only examples of the way the topics are covered in the test. The test you take will have different questions.

Score the practice questions. Go through the detailed answers in chapter 12 ("Right Answers and Explanations") and mark the questions you answered correctly and the ones you missed. Look over the explanations of the questions you missed and see if you understand them.

Decide whether you need more review. After you have looked at your results, decide if there are areas that you need to brush up on before taking the actual test. (The practice questions are grouped by topic, which may help you to spot areas of particular strength or weakness.) Go back to your textbooks and reference materials to see if the topics are covered there. You might also want to go over your questions with a friend or teacher who is familiar with the subjects.

Assess your readiness. Do you feel confident about your level of understanding in each of the subject areas? If not, where do you need more work? If you feel ready, complete the checklist in chapter 13 ("Are You Ready?") to double-check that you've thought through the details. If you need more information about registration or the testing situation itself, use the resources in Appendix B: "For More Information."

Chapter 2
Background Information on
The Praxis Series™ Assessments

▶   ▶   ▶   ▶   ▶   ▶   ▶   ▶   ▶   ▶   ▶   ▶

What are The Praxis Series Subject Assessments?

The Praxis Series Subject Assessments are designed by Educational Testing Service (ETS) to assess your knowledge of the subject area you plan to teach, and they are a part of the licensing procedure in many states. This study guide covers an assessment that tests your knowledge of the actual content you hope to be licensed to teach. Your state has adopted The Praxis Series tests because it wants to be certain that you have achieved a specified level of mastery of your subject area before it grants you a license to teach in a classroom.

The Praxis Series tests are part of a national testing program, meaning that the test covered in this study guide is used in more than one state. The advantage of taking Praxis tests is that if you want to move to another state that uses The Praxis Series tests, you can transfer your scores to that state. Passing scores are set by states, however, so if you are planning to apply for licensure in another state, you may find that passing scores are different. You can find passing scores for all states that use The Praxis Series tests in the *Understanding Your Praxis Scores* pamphlet, available either in your college's School of Education or by calling (609) 771-7395.

What is Licensure?

Licensure in any area—medicine, law, architecture, accounting, cosmetology—is an assurance to the public that the person holding the license has demonstrated a certain level of competence. The phrase used in licensure is that the person holding the license *will do no harm*. In the case of teacher licensing, a license tells the public that the person holding the license can be trusted to educate children competently and professionally.

Because a license makes such a serious claim about its holder, licensure tests are usually quite demanding. In some fields licensure tests have more than one part and last for more than one day. Candidates for licensure in all fields plan intensive study as part of their professional preparation: some join study groups, others study alone. But preparing to take a licensure test is, in all cases, a professional activity. Because it assesses your entire body of knowledge or skill for the field you want to enter, preparing for a licensure exam takes planning, discipline, and sustained effort. Studying thoroughly is highly recommended.

Why does my State Require The Praxis Series Assessments?

Your state chose The Praxis Series Assessments because the tests assess the breadth and depth of content—called the "domain" of the test—that your state wants its teachers to possess before they begin to teach. The level of content knowledge, reflected in the passing score, is based on recommendations of panels of teachers and teacher educators in each subject area in each state. The state licensing agency and, in some states, the state legislature ratify the passing scores that have been recommended by panels of teachers.

You can find out the passing score required for The Praxis Series Assessments in your state by looking in the pamphlet *Understanding Your Praxis Scores,* which is free from ETS (see above). If you look through this pamphlet, you will see that not all states use the same test modules, and even when they do, the passing scores can differ from state to state.

What Kinds of Tests are The Praxis Series Subject Assessments?

Two kinds of tests comprise The Praxis Series Subject Assessments: multiple choice (for which you select your answer from a list of choices) and constructed response (for which you write a response of your own). Multiple-choice tests can survey a wider domain because they can ask more questions in a limited period of time. Constructed-response tests have far fewer questions, but the questions require you to demonstrate the depth of your knowledge in the area covered.

What do the Tests Measure?

The Praxis Series Subject Assessments are tests of content knowledge. They measure your understanding of the subject area you want to teach. The multiple-choice tests measure a broad range of knowledge across your content area. The constructed-response tests measure your ability to explain in depth a few essential topics in your subject area. The content-specific pedagogy tests, most of which are constructed-response, measure your understanding of how to teach certain fundamental concepts in your field. The tests do not measure your actual teaching ability, however. They measure your knowledge of your subject and of how to teach it. The teachers in your field who help us design and write these tests, and the states that require these tests, do so in the belief that knowledge of subject area is the first requirement for licensing. Your teaching ability is a skill that is measured in other ways: observation, videotaped teaching, or portfolios are typically used by states to measure teaching ability. Teaching combines many complex skills, only some of which can be measured by a single test. The Praxis Series Subject Assessments are designed to measure how thoroughly you understand the material in the subject areas in which you want to be licensed to teach.

How were These Tests Developed?

ETS began the development of The Praxis Series Subject Assessments with a survey. For each subject, teachers around the country in various teaching situations were asked to judge which knowledge and skills a beginning teacher in that subject needs to possess. Professors in schools of education who prepare teachers were asked the same questions. These responses were ranked in order of importance and sent out to hundreds of teachers for review. All of the responses to these surveys (called "job analysis surveys") were analyzed to summarize the judgments of these professionals. From their consensus, we developed the specifications for the multiple-choice and constructed-response tests. Each subject area had a committee of practicing teachers and teacher educators who wrote these specifications (guidelines). The specifications were reviewed and eventually approved by teachers. From the test specifications, groups of teachers and professional test developers created test questions.

When your state adopted The Praxis Series Subject Assessments, local panels of practicing teachers and teacher educators in each subject area met to examine the tests question by question and evaluate each question for its relevance to beginning teachers in your state. This is called a "validity study." A test is considered "valid" for a job if it measures what people must know and be able to do on that job. For the test to be adopted in your state, teachers in your state must judge that it is valid.

These teachers and teacher educators also performed a "standard-setting study"; that is, they went through the tests question by question and decided, through a rigorous process, how many questions a beginning teacher should be able to answer correctly. From this study emerged a recommended passing score. The final passing score was approved by your state's Department of Education.

In other words, throughout the development process, practitioners in the teaching field—teachers and teacher educators—have determined what the tests would contain. The practitioners in your state determined which tests would be used for licensure in your subject area and helped decide what score would be needed to achieve licensure. This is how professional licensure works in most fields: those who are already licensed oversee the licensing of new practitioners. When you pass The Praxis Series Subject Assessments, you and the practitioners in your state can be assured that you have the knowledge required to begin practicing your profession.

Chapter 3

An Overview of the Study Topics for the *Social Studies: Content Knowledge* Test and the *Citizenship Education: Content Knowledge* Test

▶　▶　▶　▶　▶　▶　▶　▶　▶　▶　▶　▶

An Overview of the Study Topics for the *Social Studies: Content Knowledge* Test and the *Citizenship Education: Content Knowledge* Test

These tests focus on understanding important social, economic, cultural, and political concepts, geographical thinking, the workings of governmental systems, important historical events, and contributions of notable individuals within their historical and cultural context. The areas within social studies are mutually enriching and interdependent, and many of the questions on the test will require knowledge and integration of two or more areas.

Using the topic lists that follow: You are not expected to be an expert on the topics in the study topics chapters. But you should understand the major characteristics or aspects of each topic and be able to relate the topic to various situations presented in the test questions, e.g., a map, picture, graph, table, quotation. For instance, here is one of the topic lists in "World History," under "Disruption and Reversal (ca. 500–1400 C.E.)":

Referring to textbooks, state standards documents, and other sources as needed, make sure you can describe in your own words a brief history of Islam's origins and spread as well as the main theological and cultural differences from other belief systems. Find materials that will help you identify the major influences that Muslim learning had on the learning in other cultures (for example, in mathematics) and find the present-day locations of Islamic people. On the test you may be asked direct questions on one or more of these topics, or you may be asked to connect an aspect of Islam's history with a map, a picture, a quotation, or a comparison with another culture.

Special questions marked with stars:
Interspersed throughout the topic lists are questions that are preceded by stars (★) and outlined in boxes. These questions are intended to test your knowledge of fundamental concepts in the topic area. Some of these questions are derived from typical questions students ask, and answering them requires a significant amount of content knowledge. Other questions require you to combine several pieces of knowledge in order to formulate an integrated understanding and response. If you spend time on these questions, you will likely gain increased understanding and facility with the subject matter covered on the test.

▶ Islamic civilizations

  • Origins, beliefs, and the spread of Islam

  • Theological and cultural differences from other belief systems

  • Influence of Muslim learning on the world

  • Present-day locations of the largest populations of Islamic people

You may want to discuss these questions and your answers with a teacher or mentor.

Note that the questions marked with stars are open-ended, not multiple-choice. They are intended as *study* questions, not practice questions. Thinking about the answers to an open-ended question will improve your understanding of fundamental concepts and will probably help you answer a number of related multiple-choice questions. For example, if you do what is suggested in this starred study topic,

> ★ On your time line of United States history, take particular care with the immigration patterns in the nineteenth century, noting the decades during which immigrants from various countries or regions came to the United States in large numbers.

you have probably prepared yourself to answer the following multiple-choice question:

Immigration to the United States in the late nineteenth and early twentieth centuries differed from pre–Civil War immigration in that the groups that came later

(A) had a higher representation of people from southern and eastern Europe
(B) were generally wealthier and better educated
(C) assimilated faster and met with less prejudice
(D) were better able to escape the economic problems of some American cities

(The correct answer is (A).)

Here is an overview of the areas covered on the test, along with their sub-areas:

United States History

> Physical geography of North America
> Native American peoples
> European exploration and colonization
> Establishing a new nation (1776–1791)
> Early years of the new nation (1791–1829)
> Continued national development (1829–1850's)
> Civil War era (1850–1870's)
> Emergence of the modern United States (1877–1900)
> Progressive era through the New Deal (1900–1939)
> The Second World War and the postwar period (1939–1963)
> Recent developments (1960's–present)

World History

> Human society to approximately 3500 B.C.E.
> Development of city civilizations (ca. 3500–1500 B.C.E.)
> Ancient empires and civilizations (ca. 1500 B.C.E. – 500 C.E.)
> Disruption and reversal (ca. 500–1400 C.E.)
> Emerging global interactions (ca. 1400–1750)
> Political and industrial revolutions, nationalism (1750–1914)
> Conflicts, ideologies, and revolutions in the twentieth century
> Contemporary trends

Government and Civics

> Basic political concepts
> United States political system
> Systems of government/international politics

Geography

> The world in spatial terms
> Places and regions
> Physical systems
> Human systems
> Environment and society
> Uses of geography

Economics

> Fundamental concepts
> Microeconomics
> Macroeconomics
> International economic concepts
> Current issues and controversies

Behavioral Sciences
(not covered in the *Citizenship Education* test)

> Sociology
> Anthropology
> Psychology

Chapter 4
United States History: Study Topics

▶   ▶   ▶   ▶   ▶   ▶   ▶   ▶   ▶   ▶   ▶   ▶

United States History: Study Topics

★ Make your own timeline of United States history, starting with space for each century: 1400's, 1500's, 1600's, etc. (recognizing, of course, that Native Americans were here for thousands of years before that). Put the events listed in the study topics on your timeline in the correct century, then trace and describe in your own words important trends in cultural, intellectual, social, economic, political, and diplomatic history.

★ Other trends to identify and describe in your timeline:

★ Migration—patterns and effects

★ Technology—important developments and their effects

★ Urbanization—patterns and effects

★ Religions—dominant religions, conflicts with each other and government, influence on society and politics

★ The emergence of the United States as a world leader in the areas of military power, industry, finance, and politics

★ Explain the significance of the following dates in United States history: 1607, 1776, 1787, 1803, 1861–65, 1914–18, 1929, 1941–45

Physical geography of North America

Things to study

▶ The physical characteristics of each major region of North America

▶ Broad climate patterns of each major region of North America

▶ Location of the main geographic features of the North American continent
  • Rivers
  • Lakes
  • Mountain ranges
  • Plains
  • Deserts
  • Major United States National Parks

Native American peoples

Things to study

▶ Important points in the early political, economic, social, and cultural histories of these native North American peoples:
  • Inuit (Eskimos)
  • Anasazi (cliff dwellers)
  • Northwest Indians (Kwakiutl)
  • Plains Indians
  • Mound Builders
  • Iroquois

★ What was the Iroquois Confederation?

- Cherokee
- Seminoles

European exploration and colonization

Things to study

◗ The causes of, purposes of, and different approaches to exploration and colonization of North America by Spain, France, and England

◗ The major European explorers and the areas they each explored

★ What economic factors attracted Europeans and others to the Americas?

★ Which colonies were controlled by Spain, France, and England in North America?

◗ Interactions between the Native Americans and the Europeans

◗ Consequences of early contacts between Native Americans and Europeans (exchange of food, disease, culture, etc.)

◗ Colonial culture, society, religion, economy, and political institutions from the perspective of various inhabitants: large landowners, small farmers, artisans, women, slaves, and colonial leaders

◗ The First Great Awakening

Establishing a new nation (1776–1791)

Things to study

◗ Sources of dissatisfaction that led to the American Revolution, including the role of mercantilism and British economic policies following the French and Indian War
  - Proclamation of 1763
  - Grenville Acts, Townshend Acts, Intolerable Acts, and the tax on tea

◗ Key individuals and their roles and major ideas: King George, John Adams, George Washington, Thomas Jefferson, and Thomas Paine

◗ Major events of the war: battles of Lexington and Concord, Saratoga, Yorktown, and Treaty of Paris

◗ Major ideas in the Declaration of Independence

★ Read the Declaration of Independence carefully in its entirety if you have not already done so.

◗ The first government of the United States under the Articles of Confederation

★ What were the weaknesses in the Articles of Confederation that eventually led to its replacement by the Constitution? Why were the Articles written in this way in the first place?

◗ How the United States Constitution came into being, including major points of debates and compromises (including the Great Compromise and the Three-Fifths Compromise)

★ What were the major differences between the Federalists and Anti-Federalists?

★ What are *The Federalist* papers and what are the most important principles expressed in them?

★ Read the Constitution carefully in its entirety if you have not already done so.

◗ The addition of the Bill of Rights to the Constitution; why it was added

★ What was the position of the Founding Fathers regarding slavery?

Early years of the new nation (1791–1829)

Things to study

◗ Early presidential administrations and their challenges, including maintaining national security, creating a stable economy, court system, and defining the authority of the central government

◗ Establishment of the federal judiciary and the principle of judicial review

◗ Major disagreements between Thomas Jefferson and Alexander Hamilton and the inception and growth of political parties

◗ Economic development, including Hamilton's economic plan and tariffs

◗ Foreign policy issues and attempts to maintain neutrality: Louisiana Purchase, War of 1812, and the Monroe Doctrine

★ What were the political and economic causes and outcomes of the War of 1812?

◗ Social and cultural development in this period, including
  • Immigration
  • The frontier
  • Family life and the role of women
  • Religious life
  • Nationalism and regionalism
  • Slavery in the new nation

Continued national development (1829–1850's)

Things to study

◗ Origins of slavery in the United States, how it is addressed in the United States Constitution, and slavery's effects on political, social, religious, economic, and cultural development among African Americans and American society generally

◗ The important elements of "Jacksonian democracy" (the spoils system, veto of the National Bank, policy of American Indian removal, and opposition to the Supreme Court)

★ How did Jacksonian Democracy influence the United States social, political, and economic life?

▶ The nullification crisis (Calhoun and states' rights)

▶ Westward expansion: the Lewis and Clark expedition, the acquisition of Florida, Texas, Oregon, and California

---

★ What was "manifest destiny" and how did it influence the expansion of United States territory?

★ What was the impact of westward expansion on the United States economy?

▶ Impact of technological and agricultural innovations before the Civil War—Whitney's cotton gin, McCormick's reaper, Fulton's steamboat, and the steam locomotive; creation of a national transportation network of roads, canals, and railways

▶ Changing role of women to consumers and household managers

▶ Reasons for and consequences of waves of immigration from Europe in the first half of the nineteenth century

▶ The story of the Indian Removal Act and the "Trail of Tears," including broken treaties, massacres, conflicts, and displacement of Native Americans

▶ The Second Great Awakening and reform movements
  • Temperance
  • Prison reform
  • Early labor movement

Civil War era (1850–1870's)

Things to study

▶ The economic, philosophical, cultural, and political differences between the North, South, and West

---

★ What long-term trends or developments contributed to the growth of sectionalism?

★ How did the regions try to resolve differences? How and why did those efforts succeed or fail?

★ What were the roles of John C. Calhoun, Henry Clay, and Daniel Webster?

▶ Missouri Compromise and Compromise of 1850

▶ The abolitionist movement

★ What kinds of people were involved in the abolitionist movement, and in what ways?

★ What were the abolitionists' arguments? How did they pursue their agenda?

★ What was the impact of the abolitionists' movement on the events of the period?

▶ The Underground Railroad

▶ The women's movement

▶ The Fugitive Slave Act and the Dred Scott case

▶ Key roles and actions of Abraham Lincoln, Ulysses S. Grant, Jefferson Davis, Robert E. Lee, Frederick Douglass, William Lloyd Garrison, Harriet Tubman, Harriet Beecher Stowe, John Brown, Clara Barton

▶ Key events leading to the declaration of secession and war

▶ Significance of the most major events during the war: capture of Fort Sumter, battles of Gettysburg and Vicksburg, the destruction of Atlanta, Lee's final surrender

★ What were the advantages that each side, the North and the South, enjoyed before the war began? What were each side's disadvantages? How did these shift during the war?

▶ Major points and provisions in the Gettysburg Address, the Emancipation Proclamation, the 13th, 14th, and 15th Amendments to the United States Constitution

▶ Development and impact of Reconstruction policies on the South and the Compromise of 1877, Jim Crow laws

★ What did Reconstruction plans and policies accomplish, and where did they fail?

★ What were the short- and long-term effects of the Compromise of 1877?

Emergence of the modern United States (1877–1900)

Things to study

▶ Displacement of Native Americans from western lands

▶ Segregation after the Civil War, including the Supreme Court decision in *Plessy v. Ferguson*

▶ Business and labor after the Civil War
  • Tariffs, banking, land grants, and subsidies and how states and the federal government used them to encourage business expansion
  • Bankers and entrepreneurs Andrew Carnegie, John D. Rockefeller, and J. P. Morgan: their industries and the changes in American business that they represented
  • The dominance of sharecropping in the South
  • The state of urban areas, especially those affected by renewed immigration, migration from rural areas, difficult working conditions (including child labor), and greater social stratification

★ What conditions and problems are portrayed in Upton Sinclair's novel *The Jungle*?

  • The beginnings of the labor movement, including the views and actions of Samuel Gompers, the Knights of Labor, and the American Federation of Labor

▶ Asian and European immigration

★ What were the "push" and "pull" factors that contributed to late-nineteenth-century immigration to the United States?

★ On your timeline of United States history, take particular care with the immigration patterns in the nineteenth century, noting the decades during which immigrants from various countries or regions came to the United States in large numbers.

★ Late-nineteenth-century immigration to the United States can be viewed in terms of creating a "melting pot" or a "pluralist" or "multicultural" society. What does this distinction mean, and why is it important?

▶ The Pendleton Act

▶ The Muckrakers

▶ Political, cultural, and social movements, including the Populist movement, Social Darwinism, women's rights, and the Social Gospel

★ What reforms did Susan B. Anthony, W. E. B. DuBois, and Robert LaFollette lead?

★ Compare and contrast Populism and Progressivism.

▶ America's imperialism at the turn of the century as evidenced in the Spanish-American War, the building of the Panama Canal, and Theodore Roosevelt's "Big Stick" diplomacy, and the Open Door policy

Progressive era through the New Deal (1900–1939)

Things to study

▶ Political and social reforms, direct ballot, settlement-house movement

▶ Internal migration and Mexican immigration

▶ America's role in the First World War and postwar isolationism

▶ Major actions by Woodrow Wilson

▶ The League of Nations

▶ Important developments in the 1920's
 • The Harlem Renaissance (Zora Neale Hurston, Langston Hughes)
 • Prohibition
 • Women's suffrage (the movement and the amendment)
 • The rise of mass-production techniques and new technologies with far-reaching effects (e.g., automobile and electricity)
 • Immigration and the National Origins Act

▶ The Great Depression and the New Deal
 • Causes of the Depression
 • Impact of the Depression on various groups in the United States
 • Franklin D. Roosevelt and the New Deal (Works Progress Administration; Social Security; National Labor Relations Board)

★ What were the major successes, failures, and legacies of the New Deal?

The Second World War and the postwar period (1939–1963)

Things to study

◆ America's role in the Second World War and consequences at home and abroad
  - Attack on Pearl Harbor
  - Battles of Midway, Iwo Jima, Okinawa, and the invasion of Normandy
  - Internment of Japanese Americans
  - Decision to drop atomic bombs on Hiroshima and Nagasaki and the consequences

---

★ How might history have been different if the United States had decided not to drop the atomic bombs?

◆ America's role in the Cold War, major provisions of the Marshall Plan

◆ Korean War—major causes and outcomes

◆ Important political, economic, social, and cultural events and trends in the 1950's, including *Brown* v. *Board of Education of Topeka,* the "American dream," the baby boom, the GI Bill, rise of suburbia, and growth of consumer society

◆ Red Scare and McCarthyism

◆ Cuban missile crisis

Recent developments (1960's–Present)

Things to study

◆ Vietnam War—major causes, events, and outcomes; student protests in the United States

◆ African American Civil Rights movement; the leadership and assassination of Martin Luther King Jr.

◆ The women's movement, peace movement, migrant farm workers movement, and environmentalism movement

◆ Social policy initiatives: the "Great Society" and the "War on Poverty"

◆ Watergate scandal

◆ Increase in the number of working women and changes in family structure

◆ Changing demographics—subcultures and ethnic and cultural identities

◆ Conservative movements—religious conservatives, tax revolts, the drive to reduce the size of government

◆ Industrial trends—the decline of unions; the growth of the service sector; the growth of the budget deficit; the impact of deregulation; energy and environmental issues

◆ International relations, including United States relations with the Soviet Union and its successor states and the changing role of the United States in world political and economic affairs

◆ Development of computers and information systems and their impact on the economy and jobs

Chapter 5
World History: Study Topics

▶　　▶　　▶　　▶　　▶　　▶　　▶　　▶　　▶　　▶　　▶　　▶

World History: Study Topics

★ Work with a globe or world map as you study and review world history. It would be especially useful to use a historical atlas so that you can see a place or region in its historical context. In addition, many recent world history textbooks have excellent maps. Find regions and places you are studying on the globe and make sure you understand the locations, movements, and relationships among the many societies you are reviewing.

★ Think carefully about the periods into which this history is divided. You will probably find alternative schemes—that is, different names and year spans—in the materials you use for review. Why do historians divide history into periods? Do they agree on the names and dates of some periods more than others? What do the periods say about historical interpretation? How do periods relate to long-term trends?

★ Explain the significance of the following dates in world history: 220 C.E. and 476 C.E., 622 C.E., 1096-1099 C.E., 1200–1300, 1453, 1492, 1750–1780, 1789, 1870's, 1914–18, 1939–45, 1947, 1957, 1989. (If you cannot find these on your own, see the list at the end of this chapter.)

Human society to approximately 3500 B.C.E.

Things to study

▶ Major characteristics of human societies during the Paleolithic and Neolithic periods, with special concentration on hunter-gatherer societies and the agricultural revolution

▶ Development of settled societies, specialization of tasks, toolmaking, and the emergence of agriculture

Development of city civilizations (ca. 3500–1500 B.C.E.)

Things to study

▶ Locations, major characteristics, and major contributions (architectural monuments, writing, technological capabilities) of the following ancient civilizations:
  • Mesopotamia (ca. 3500–ca. 2350 B.C.E.) (writing, military expertise, city–states, Code of Hammurabi)
  • Egypt (ca. 3000–ca. 1550 B.C.E.) (hieroglyphics, the Rosetta Stone, pyramids, religious rulership)
  • Indus River Valley (ca. 2500–ca. 1750 B.C.E.) (importance of water, city planning, agriculture)
  • Early China (ca. 1700–ca. 771 B.C.E.) (writing, ancestor worship, manorialism)
  • Olmec society in Mesoamerica (ca. 1200–ca. 400 B.C.E.) (monumental sculpture, ceremonial centers, writing)

Ancient empires and civilizations (ca. 1500 B.C.E.–500 C.E.)

Things to study

- Egypt (ca. 1552–ca. 1070 B.C.E.)
  - Influence of geography on the civilization
  - Pyramids and the Valley of Kings
  - Important contributions in art, writing, architecture

- Greece (ca. 2000–ca. 300 B.C.E.)
  - Influence of geography on the civilization
  - Social structure and the concepts of citizenship and democracy
    - Contrasting views of society: Athens and Sparta

> ★ How were the concepts of citizenship and democracy in ancient Greece similar and different from contemporary United States concepts of citizenship and democracy?

- Commerce, the city-state, and colonies
- Persian Wars and Peloponnesian Wars
- Alexander the Great and the spread of Greek ideas
- Important contributions (in drama, sculpture, sports, architecture, mathematics, and science) and the emphasis on human achievement

- Rome (ca. 700 B.C.E.–500 C.E.)
  - Influence of geography on the civilization
  - Military domination, and its impact on the economy and society
  - Extent of the empire at key points

> ★ How big did the Roman Empire get, with what borders, at its largest? In comparison, how small was it when it fell? What were the main reasons for the success at its largest point and its gradual shrinking?

- Government of Rome: republic to empire
- The establishment of "rule by law" and the concept of citizenship
- Roles of Julius and Augustus Caesar
- Characteristics of the Pax Romana
- Origin and spread of Christianity, including Constantine's role
- Important contributions in the areas of architecture, technology, science, literature, history, law, military science, and engineering
- Major causes for the decline and fall of the empire

- India
  - Aryan conquest of the Ganges Valley
  - Caste system

> ★ Does the caste system survive in India today? How has the caste system shaped India's social, cultural, economic, and political histories?

- Hinduism and Buddhism (origins, beliefs)

- China
  - Imperial government by trained bureaucracy
  - Taoism, Confucianism, Buddhism
  - The Great Wall, printing, compass, paper, gunpowder
  - Significance and consequences of China's insularity

- Japan
  - Effects of geographic isolation and relationship with China
  - Shinto and Buddhism
  - Emperors, shoguns, and samurai

★ What are the fundamental ideas and institutions that arose from the cultures of India, China, and Japan?

★ What are the fundamental ideas and institutions that arose from the cultures of Egypt, Greece, and Rome?

★ Consider whether the terms "Eastern" and "Western" help or hinder understanding of developments in this period.

Disruption and reversal (ca. 500–1400 C.E.)

Things to study

◗ Nomadic migrations: Huns to Mongols

◗ Location and culture of the Byzantine Empire

◗ Islamic civilizations
  • Origins, beliefs, and spread of Islam
  • Theological and cultural differences from other belief systems
  • Influence of Muslim learning on the world
  • Present-day locations of the largest populations of Islamic people

★ What has been the role of Islam in African history?

★ What have been the most important ways that the Islamic world has influenced European history?

◗ Economic, social, and political effects of feudalism in Europe and Japan

◗ Conflicts among Eurasian powers: the Crusades, the Mongol conquests, Ottoman conquests

◗ The Black Death, its spread, and its impact on the global population

◗ Central and South America
  • Mayans
  • Aztecs
  • Incas
  • Exchange of food, diseases, and culture between Europeans and Native Americans in the Americas, and later, exchange of products and African slaves

★ Why were the Spanish able to defeat the Aztec and Inca empires?

◗ Sub-Saharan Africa
  • Trading empires
  • Forest kingdoms

Emerging global interactions (ca. 1400–1750)

Things to study

◗ Transition from subsistence agriculture and feudalism to market economies

◗ Early navigational advancements and discoveries and their consequences and implications

◗ Chinese voyages in the Indian Ocean

◗ European voyages of Magellan, Christopher Columbus, Vasco da Gama

◗ Patterns of cultural contact, including the disruption of African culture by slavery and imperialism, the rejection of European culture by China and Japan, and the conquest of Mesoamerica

◆ Renaissance
- Link between the Renaissance and the Islamic world
- New trade and economic practices that gave rise to the wealth of Italian city-states
- Contributions to the arts and sciences

★ How did the artistic, literary, and intellectual creativity of the Renaissance, including that of da Vinci, Michelangelo, and Shakespeare, contrast with the creativity during the medieval period?

◆ Reformation

◆ Scientific Revolution: scientific theories and discoveries by Newton, Copernicus, and Galileo

★ How did the Scientific Revolution change the way humans perceived themselves and the universe, and how did it change the methods of human inquiry?

◆ Enlightenment
- Major ideas that characterized Enlightenment thought; major theoretical contributions of Locke, Voltaire, and Rousseau
- How the political ideas of the Enlightenment affected the American, French, and Latin American Revolutions

Political and Industrial Revolutions, Nationalism (1750–1914)

Things to study

◆ Industrial Revolution
- Rise of industrial economies in the late 1700's and early 1800's, especially in England, and their link to imperialism and colonization in the nineteenth century
- How scientific and technological changes brought about massive social and cultural changes
- The factory system

★ Why was England the birthplace of the Industrial Revolution?

★ How did the banking system as it developed in the 1400's through the 1700's enable the Industrial Revolution to thrive?

◆ The French Revolution and its impact

◆ Latin American independence movements

◆ New ideologies, including liberalism, socialism, and Marxism

◆ Nationalist and imperialist ideologies and movements
- Revolutions of the 1830's and 1848
- The unifications of Italy and Germany
- European imperialism
  - European colonies in Asia and Africa at the end of the nineteenth century
  - How Asia and Africa have been transformed by European commercial power
  - China's resistance and revolution
  - The Meiji Restoration of Japan

Conflicts, ideologies, and evolutions in the twentieth century

Things to study

▶ Causes of, major events in, and consequences of the First World War

---

★ Why was the First World War followed by the emergence of a number of totalitarian governments?

▶ Revolutions: Russian, Mexican, and Chinese Revolutions

★ What do the French and Russian revolutions have in common?

▶ The impact of the First World War on colonialism

▶ Worldwide economic depression in the 1930's and the political, social, and economic impact

▶ Rise of communism in the Soviet Union and China; the rise of fascism in Germany, Italy, and Japan

▶ Influence and actions of Lenin, Stalin, Mao Zedong, Adolf Hitler, Franklin Roosevelt, Mohandas Gandhi, Kwame Nkrumah, Nelson Mandela

▶ Causes of and consequences of the Second World War; the Allied and Axis powers

▶ The Holocaust

▶ Post-Second World War alliances and associations

- Origin and meaning of the Cold War; containment policies in Europe, Latin America, and Asia
- NATO
- Warsaw Pact
- European Economic Community
- Organization of African Unity
- OPEC
- SEATO

▶ The creation of the modern Middle East from the Ottoman Empire

▶ Post-Second World War China: the Great Leap Forward, the Cultural Revolution, political control, and the move to a market economy

▶ Post-Second World War Soviet Union
- Repression of movements for independence (Hungary, Poland, Czechoslovakia)
- Gorbachev: perestroika and glasnost
- Dissolution of the Soviet Union

▶ Economic and military power shifts since 1945, including reasons for the rise of Germany and Japan

▶ Post-Second World War decolonization in Africa and Asia and increased democracy in Europe, and elsewhere, including
- India and Pakistan in 1947
- Sub-Saharan nations in the 1960's and 1970's
- The Philippines in the 1980's
- Nations in Eastern Europe, Balkans, and the former Soviet Union in the 1980's and 1990's

▶ Rise of a global culture

★ What are the main reasons that a global culture emerged in the late twentieth century? What are the major elements and the consequences of this global culture?

▶ Rise of a global economy

▶ Major scientific advances: atomic bomb, atomic power, space travel, satellite technology, computers

Contemporary trends

Things to study

▶ "New Europe"

▶ Emergence of the "Pacific Rim"

▶ Regional and global economic and environmental interdependence

▶ Spread of Western culture and reactions to it: the making of a global culture

▶ The welfare state and liberation movements; feminism, oppressed minorities, and oppressed classes

▶ New challenges: genetic manipulation, Internet, e-commerce

Significance of dates listed on p. 31.

220 and 476	Fall of Han dynasty and fall of western Roman Empire
622	Flight of Muhammad to Medina (considered the beginning of Islam)
1096–1099	The First Crusade
1200–1300	Mongol domination of Asia
1453	The Fall of Constantinople to the Ottomans
1492	Columbus lands in the Americas
1750–1780	Height of the Atlantic slave trade
1789	The French Revolution
1870's	Scramble for Africa begins
1914–18	The First World War
1939–45	The Second World War
1947	Independence of India and Pakistan
1957	Sputnik launched
1989	Fall of the Berlin Wall

Chapter 6

Government and Civics: Study Topics

▶ ▶ ▶ ▶ ▶ ▶ ▶ ▶ ▶ ▶ ▶ ▶

Government and Civics: Study Topics

Basic political concepts

Things to study

- Reasons why government is needed (conflict resolution, collective decision-making, etc.); how governments are created and changed

- Political theory and major theorists such as Machiavelli, Hobbes, Locke, Marx, and Lenin

---

★ What are the main ideas of each theorist as they contribute to the development of forms of government and their institutions?

★ For example, where did the ideas of sovereignty and social contract found in the United States Constitution come from?

★ Where did the concepts of checks and balances and the separation of powers come from?

★ How did the concepts of Marx and Lenin influence various forms of governments in the twentieth century?

- Major political concepts such as citizenship, legitimacy, power, justice, authority, liberty, majoritarianism, rights and responsibilities, federalism, and sovereignty

- Political orientations: radical, liberal, conservative, and reactionary

---

★ What are the core ideas of each political orientation?

★ What sorts of government or policy would be supported by each, and why?

United States political system

Things to study

- The content and structure of the United States Constitution and the Bill of Rights, and the ongoing processes of constitutional interpretation and amendment

- The "separation of powers" among the three branches of the federal government and the major responsibilities of each branch

---

★ What are the intended functions of checks and balances and the separation of powers? What have been the actual outcomes—how does it really work?

★ What are the formal powers of each branch, how are they applied, and how have the branches tried to get around the checks on their power?

★ What are the real-life policy consequences of the institutional arrangements under the Constitution?

- Various functions and processes in the federal government
  - Regulatory functions controlled by various government agencies
  - Executive branch functions in the Departments of Agriculture, Commerce, Defense, Education, Energy, etc.
  - Impeachment process

- Process for ratifying a treaty
- Electoral College
- Line of authority if the president and vice president are incapacitated

▶ The formation and operation of political institutions not established by the Constitution, such as political parties, political action committees, interest groups, and the federal bureaucracy; also, the role of the media and public opinion in American political life

▶ Relationships among federal, state, and local governments

★ What impact do these relationships have on policy, responsibility, and authority? How have the relationships developed and changed over time? What factors drove those changes?

▶ Regulatory commissions such as the Federal Communications Commission

▶ Individual and group political behavior, including voting behavior, changes in group opinion over time, interactions of race, class, and gender with political participation and opinion, and forms of political participation

▶ Hierarchy of the federal court system

▶ Landmark Supreme Court decisions, such as
- *Marbury* v. *Madison*
- *McCulloch* v. *Maryland*
- *Scott* v. *Sandford*
- *Plessy* v. *Ferguson*
- *Brown* v. *Board of Education of Topeka*
- *Miranda* v. *Arizona*
- *Roe* v. *Wade*
- *Gibbons* v. *Ogden*
- *Regents of the University of California* v. *Bakke*
- *Reynolds* v. *Sims*
- *United States* v. *Virginia (VMI)*

▶ Judicial activism *versus* judicial restraint

Systems of government/ international politics

Things to study

▶ Forms of government
- Classical republic
- Liberal democracy
- Federalism
- Absolute monarchy
- Dictatorship
- Parliamentary system
- Autocracy, oligarchy, theocracy, plutocracy

▶ International relations in theory and practice (diplomacy, conflict, cooperation)

▶ Functions, powers, problems of international organizations and international law (human rights, world health, democratization)

Chapter 7
Geography: Study Topics

▶ ▶ ▶ ▶ ▶ ▶ ▶ ▶ ▶ ▶ ▶ ▶

Geography: Study Topics

The World in spatial terms

Things to study

◗ Longitude and latitude and their purposes

◗ Geographic features (landforms) that make up Earth (continents, oceans, seas, rivers, bays, mountain ranges, plateaus, valleys, plains, ice caps, tundra, forest, grassland, desert, island)

◗ Location of the seven continents, the four oceans, major seas and rivers, major mountain ranges, the equator, the prime meridian, and the international date line

---

★ Be able to read and interpret different kinds of maps and images (physical, topographical, political, and weather maps; aerial photographs and satellite images).

★ Be able to use map legends to estimate distances, calculate scale, identify patterns represented in maps, and compute population density.

★ What is "map projection" and what kinds of decisions does it force mapmakers to make?

◗ General climate patterns for major parts of each continent

◗ Mental maps and their use as a way of organizing information about people, places, and environments in a spatial context

Places and regions

Things to study

◗ Location of major regions, countries, and cities of the world

◗ Ways in which regions are categorized (e.g., political, physical, cultural)

★ What are the primary characteristics of each of these regions, and why? North Africa/Southwest Asia, Sub-Saharan Africa, Latin America, the Caribbean, North America, Western Europe, Eastern Europe, East Asia, South Asia, Southeast Asia, and Oceania

---

Physical systems

Things to study

◗ The fundamental forces at work in weather systems, climate, and seasonal changes

---

★ What is the difference between weather and climate?

★ How do each of the following factors influence climate? Latitude, ocean currents, winds, mountains, elevation, proximity to water

★ What is El Niño?

◗ The basic mechanisms and consequences of physical changes that have short-term effects on Earth, including floods, droughts, and snowstorms

▶ The basic mechanisms and consequences of physical changes that have long-term effects on Earth, including earthquakes (plate tectonics) and natural erosion

★ Where do most earthquakes occur currently, and why?

★ Know what an ecosystem is and why understanding ecosystems is important.

Human systems

Things to study

▶ Factors affecting settlement patterns—why some places are densely populated and others sparsely populated

▶ Major cultural characteristics in the largest regions and nations in the world

★ Be able to read and interpret "population pyramids."

▶ Population movements: basic concepts (push, pull factors); major trends in the population patterns in the world in the nineteenth and twentieth centuries and their causes (e.g., the Great Irish Famine)

★ What regions of the United States grew faster than others in the twentieth century? Why?

★ What are the major trends in ethnic composition of the United States population in the twentieth and twenty-first centuries?

▶ Distinctions between developing and developed (industrialized) nations; the relative wealth of the most populous nations

▶ Major trade relationships, especially those between the United States and other nations in the late twentieth and early twenty-first centuries; economic interdependence among major regions and nations in the late twentieth century

▶ Concepts related to the "Human Systems" category
- Central-place theory
- Density thresholds
- Diffusion theory

Environment and society

Things to study

▶ The impact of the environment on human systems such as
- Essentials like food, clothing, and shelter
- Transportation and recreation
- Economic and industrial systems

★ How has the wide range of climate zones in Latin America influenced the history of the region?

★ How has the limited supply of water influenced the historical and economic development of the Middle East?

▶ Effects of human-initiated changes on the environment and community
- Water, air, and ground pollution
- Deforestation and desertification
- Global warming
- Ozone depletion

★ How did major human alterations of the landscape such as the Panama and Suez Canals affect economic, political, and cultural history?

◗ Natural resources—what they are and why they matter
- Renewable and nonrenewable resources
- Energy, mineral, food, and land resources

★ Name some changes that have occurred in the twentieth century in the use, distribution, and importance of natural resources.

Uses of Geography

Things to study

◗ Apply geography to interpret the past

◗ Apply geography to interpret the present and plan for the future

★ Think about how geography can be a helpful component when interpreting past or present events or situations such as

The origins of the Industrial Revolution

Decisions made by the United States government in the nineteenth century concerning Native Americans

The political situations in Korea in the 1940's and 1950's and Vietnam in the 1960's and 1970's

The current conflicts in the Middle East

Chapter 8
Economics: Study Topics

▶   ▶   ▶   ▶   ▶   ▶   ▶   ▶   ▶   ▶   ▶   ▶

Economics: Study Topics

Fundamental concepts

Things to study

▶ Be able to analyze how limited productive resources force nations and individuals to deal with the issues of choice and cost.

▶ Production possibility models are used to describe the economic issues of scarcity, choice, and cost. Using the production possibility, you then should be able to explain the concepts of absolute and comparative advantage and the reasons for trade among nations and individuals.

▶ You should be able to compare and contrast generally how differing economic systems of command, mixed, and market economies attempt to deal with the economic problem.

▶ Finally, you should know the basic institutions that compose the market economy. The circular-flow model is used to examine the relationships among individual households, firms, government, and the foreign sector.

Key conceptual questions:

▶ Scarcity and the nature of economic systems

> ★ Why does the problem of scarcity force people to consider opportunity cost?

▶ Opportunity cost and the production possibilities model

> ★ What does a production possibilities curve demonstrate?

▶ The basis for trade: absolute and comparative advantage and the role of specialization

> ★ Why do people engage in exchange?
>
> ★ What are the sources of gain from trade?

▶ Types and functions of economic systems: command, market, and mixed economies

> ★ What are the methods of economic organization? How do they differ?

▶ Basic economic institutions of a market economy (households, firms, resource markets and product markets, foreign markets)

> ★ How does the circular-flow model describe the operation of the market economy?

Microeconomics

Things to study

▶ You should know the determinants of supply and demand and the ways in which changes in these determinants affect equilibrium price and output. Further analysis of supply and demand requires an understanding of how government impacts demand and supply models through the use of taxation, subsidies, price floors, and ceilings.

▶ You should also study the instances under which the private market may fail to allocate resources efficiently, as in the case of negative or positive externalities. Understand the characteristics and behavior of the product markets known as perfect competition and monopoly. By comparing and contrasting perfect competition with monopoly, you should be able to evaluate the efficiency of the two market models.

▶ Understand the resource markets, focusing primarily on labor. Be able to extend and apply the mechanics of supply and demand models to labor markets, and be able to explain the impact of labor union activities and governmental policy on wages and employment.

Key conceptual questions:

▶ Supply and demand, equilibrium price and quantity determination, and basic manipulation of supply and demand as well as the impacts of price ceilings and floors, taxes and externalities

★ What are the laws of supply and demand?

★ How is the market price of a good determined?

★ How do markets adjust to changes in demand? How do markets adjust to changes in supply?

★ What happens when prices are set above the market equilibrium price? What happens when prices are set below the market equilibrium price?

★ How does the imposition of a tax affect a market?

▶ Product markets: comparison and contrast of price and output in perfect competition and price and output in monopoly

★ What are the characteristics of a perfect competition and of a monopoly? Compare and contrast in terms of
  The number of buyers and sellers
  The type of product sold
  Degree of control over price
  Conditions of entry
  Efficiency (allocative and productive)

★ How do government policies attempt to regulate pure competition and monopolies?

▶ Factors markets, labor, land, capital, the determination of wages and employment, and the distribution of income

★ Why do business fir... machines, and othe...

★ What determines t... resource such as la...

★ Why do some pe... others do?

★ Can the unions... all workers?

★ What is the effe... law on wages an... labor markets?

Macroeconomics

Things to study

▶ Be familiar with basic macroeconomic concepts, including gross national product (GNP) and gross domestic product (GDP), inflation, and unemployment. Understand the components that make up GDP and the problems of calculating GDP. Understand the use of consumer price index (CPI) as a measure of the price level and the role of the CPI in making distinctions between nominal and real income values.

▶ After you understand national output, then turn to the basic models of aggregate demand (AD) and aggregate supply (AS) and how the AS/AD model determines the equilibrium level of GDP. Be aware of the classical and Keynesian contributions to the understanding of the AS/AD model. (You will be required to use AS/AD models to describe various

...e economy, including ...essions, stagflation,

...your understanding of the fiscal ... tools available to government ...ers. Be able to evaluate the use ...monetary tools to achieve price ...ployment, and growth.

...ual questions:

...of economic performance, gross ...roduct (GNP), gross domestic ...GDP): the GDP, the consumer ...ex (including calculation and ...tation and conversion of nominal ...alues), and macroeconomic goals, including price stability, employment, and growth

★ What is gross domestic product (GDP)? What are the major components of GDP?

★ What is a price index? What do price indexes measure? How can they be used to adjust for changes in the general level of prices?

▶ Aggregate Supply and Aggregate Demand models (price and output determination; basic manipulation of aggregate supply and aggregate demand)
  • Evaluation of economy (inflation, recessions, depressions, stagflations)
  • Role of fiscal policy (government spending and taxation policies)
  • Role of monetary policy, including the purpose and functions of the Federal Reserve (FED), the FED's tools, including open-market operations, reserve requirements, and discount rates

★ What determines the equilibrium level of GDP of any economy?

★ What factors cause shifts in aggregate demand? What factors cause shifts in the aggregate supply?

★ How does the economy adjust to changes in aggregate supply and/or aggregate demand?

★ What are the causes of recessions and booms (periods of inflation)?

★ How does fiscal policy affect aggregate demand and/or aggregate supply?

★ What are the major functions of the Federal Reserve System?

★ What are the major tools of the Federal Reserve to control the supply of money?

★ What are the appropriate fiscal or monetary policies to deal with
      Inflation
      Depressions/recessions
      Stagflation

International economic concepts

Things to study

▶ Understand why the reasons for international trade are given through the study of absolute and comparative advantage.

▶ Understand why the motive for international trade leads to other issues, including currency exchange rates and balance of payments, which in turn affect a country's price levels,

employment, and level of output. Understand the significance of trade restrictions, tariffs, and quotas, as they affect domestic policy goals.

Key conceptual questions:

▶ International trade (absolute and comparative advantages, trade balance, exchange rates and balance of payments)
- Effects of international trade (net exports) on the domestic economy
- International currency fluctuation, appreciation and depreciation of a nation's currency and its effect on net exports and capital flows
- Pros and cons of protectionist policy

★ Why do nations trade? When can a nation gain from international trade?

★ Why do nations impose trade restrictions? What impact do trade restrictions have on the economy?

★ What determines the exchange rate of the United States dollar in the foreign-exchange market?

★ What information is provided in the balance of payments account?

★ How does fiscal and/or monetary policy affect exchange rates and/or the balance of payments?

★ How do net exports influence the domestic economy in terms of output, price level, and employment?

Current issues and controversies

<u>Things to study</u>

▶ You should look for discussions of current issues in economics textbooks as well as in newspaper articles. Questions will test your understanding of economic controversies surrounding issues such as those below:

- The balanced-budget amendment
- The protectionist arguments for tariffs, quotas, and restrictive immigration policies
- The use and effectiveness of the minimum-wage laws
- Government regulation of industry
- Protecting the environment versus stimulating economic growth
- The relative effectiveness of fiscal and monetary policy

Chapter 9

Behavioral Sciences: Study Topics

▶   ▶   ▶   ▶   ▶   ▶   ▶   ▶   ▶   ▶   ▶   ▶

Behavioral Sciences: Study Topics

Note: The topics in this chapter are **not** covered in the *Citizenship Education: Content Knowledge* test. If you are required to take the *Citizenship Education: Content Knowledge* test, you do not need to study this chapter.

Sociology

Things to study

▶ Basic concepts in sociology
- Networks
- Primary and secondary groups
- Social solidarity and conflict
- Role
- Status
- Norms
- Minorities, ethnicity
- Group
- Institutions

▶ Socialization
- The role of socialization in society
- Major agents of socialization
- The roles of positive and negative sanctions in the socialization process

▶ Patterns of social organization
- The concept of role
- The functions of primary and secondary groups and of group norms
- Folkways, mores, laws, beliefs, and values
- Conformity and deviance
- Social stratification
- Social mobility

▶ Social institutions—family, education, government, faith communities, clubs, ethnic communities, sports organizations and their visible outgrowths (customs, symbols, celebrations)

▶ Study of populations—the impact on society of changes in population growth and distribution, migration, and immigration

▶ Multicultural diversity
- The concepts of ethnocentrism, stereotypes, biases, values, ideals, prejudice, and cultural relativity
- The prevalence and consequences of prejudice and discrimination
- The concepts of pluralism and multicultural diversity

▶ Social problems—contemporary social problems, including causes, consequences, and proposed solutions

Anthropology

Things to study

▶ Basic goals of anthropology and archaeology

▶ The two branches of anthropology: physical and cultural

▶ Human culture
- The process of enculturation by which societal roles are learned
- The societal functions of language and communication
- Social stratification
- The functioning of subcultures within dominant cultures

★ What are some of the major subcultures in the United States?

★ What are some cultural norms of each of these subcultures?

★ What are some stereotypes that others hold about each of these subcultures?

▶ How cultures change—invention, innovation, cultural diffusion, adaptation, acculturation, assimilation, retention, reinterpretation, and extinction

Psychology

Things to study

▶ Foundational theories
  - Major ideas in learning theory, cognitive theory, behavioral psychology, humanistic psychology, and abnormal psychology
  - Major contributions of Sigmund Freud, Carl Jung, Jean Piaget, Ivan Pavlov, B. F. Skinner, and Erik Erickson

▶ Basic concepts and approaches
  - Cognitive development
  - Behavioralism
  - Physiological influences
  - Social influences
  - Emotions
  - Personality
  - Self-concept
  - Motives
  - Values
  - Perception

▶ Human growth and development
  - Four stages (infancy, childhood, adolescence, adulthood)
  - Physical, cognitive, social, and emotional development

▶ Personality and adjustment
  - Theories of personality, self-esteem, adjustment, motivation, and assessment
  - Intervention and prevention in dealing with adjustment problems and exceptional behavior common in the classroom

▶ Abnormal psychology
  - Common psychological disorders and their major symptoms

▶ Social psychology—group processes, attitudes, and social cognition

Chapter 10

Don't Be Defeated by
Multiple-Choice Questions

▶ ▶ ▶ ▶ ▶ ▶ ▶ ▶ ▶ ▶ ▶ ▶

Why the Multiple-Choice Tests Take Time

When you take the practice questions, you will see that there are very few simple identification questions of the "Which of the following authors wrote *Moby Dick*?" sort. When The Praxis Series™ Assessments were first being developed by teachers and teacher educators across the country, it was almost universally agreed that prospective teachers should be able to analyze situations, synthesize material, and apply knowledge to specific examples. In short, they should be able to think as well as to recall specific facts, figures, or formulas. Consequently, you will find that you are being asked to think and to solve problems on your test. Such activity takes more time than simply answering identification questions.

In addition, questions that require you to analyze situations, synthesize material, and apply knowledge are usually longer than are simple identification questions. The Praxis Series test questions often present you with something to read (a case study, a sample of student work, a chart or graph) and ask you questions based on your reading. Strong reading skills are required, and you must read carefully. Both on this test and as a teacher, you will need to process and use what you read efficiently.

If you know your reading skills are not strong, you may want to take a reading course. College campuses have reading labs that can help you strengthen your reading skills.

Understanding Multiple-Choice Questions

You will probably notice that the word order in multiple-choice questions (or syntax) is different from the word order you're used to seeing in ordinary things you read, like newspapers or textbooks. One of the reasons for this difference is that many such questions contain the phrase "which of the following."

The purpose of the phrase "which of the following" is to limit your choice of answers only to the list given. For example, look at this question.

> Which of the following is a flavor made from beans?
> (A) Strawberry
> (B) Cherry
> (C) Vanilla
> (D) Mint

You may know that chocolate and coffee are flavors made from beans also. But they are not listed, and the question asks you to select from among the list that follows ("which of the following"). So the answer has to be the only bean-derived flavor in the list: vanilla.

Notice that the answer can be submitted for the phrase "which of the following." In the question above, you could insert "vanilla" for "which of the following" and have the sentence "Vanilla is a flavor made from beans." Sometimes it helps to cross out "which of the following" and insert the various choices. You may want to give this technique a try as you answer various multiple-choice questions in the practice test.

Also, looking carefully at the "which of the following" phrase helps you to focus on what the question is asking you to find and on the answer choices. In the simple example above, all of the answer choices are flavors. Your job is to decide which of the flavors is the one made from beans.

The vanilla bean question is pretty straightforward. But the phrase "which of the following" can also be found in more challenging questions. Look at this question:

The population pyramid of a population that has had a slightly larger birth rate than death rate for several generations will most likely have which of the following shapes?

(A) Wider at the top than in the middle

(B) Wider at the bottom than at the top

(C) Bulging in the middle

(D) Having parallel sides

The placement of "which of the following" tells you that the list of choices is a list of "shapes." What are you supposed to find as an answer? You are supposed to find the choice that describes the shape of a population pyramid that reflects a higher birth rate than death rate.

Sometimes it helps to put the question in your own words. Here, you could paraphrase the question as "If there are more births than deaths, what would the pyramid look like?" A pattern of larger birth rate than death rate would produce greater numbers of people in the younger age categories than in the older age categories. This means that the population pyramid would be increasingly broad at its base, making (B) the correct answer.

You may find that it helps you to circle or underline each of the critical details of the question in your test book so that you don't miss any of them. It's only by looking at all parts of the question carefully that you will have all of the information you need to answer the question.

Circle or underline the critical parts of what is being asked in this question.

Which of the following best summarizes the attitude of most delegates to the United States Constitutional Convention in 1787 toward the development of political parties?

(A) Parties would be beneficial to the growth of democracy.

(B) Parties would eventually return the country to dependence on Great Britain because they are suggestive of rule by monarchy.

(C) Parties would divide the country into hostile camps and would be disruptive to the conduct of political affairs.

(D) Parties would ensure that the delegates would control the government of the new nation.

Here is one possible way you may have annotated the question:

Which of the following best summarizes the (attitude) of most <u>delegates</u> to the United States <u>Constitutional Convention in 1787</u> toward the development of <u>political parties</u>?

(A) Parties would be beneficial to the growth of democracy.

(B) Parties would eventually return the country to dependence on Great Britain because they are suggestive of rule by monarchy.

(C) Parties would divide the country into hostile camps and would be disruptive to the conduct of political affairs.

(D) Parties would ensure that the delegates would control the government of the new nation.

After spending a minute with the question, you can probably see that you are being asked to recognize what most delegates at the 1787 Convention thought about political parties. (The answer is (C).) The important thing is understanding what the question is asking. With enough practice, you should be able to determine what any question is asking. Knowing the answer is, of course, a different matter, but you have to understand a question before you can answer it.

It takes more work to understand "which of the following" questions when there are even more words in a question. Questions that require application or interpretation invariably require extra reading.

Consider this question.

> "While we abhor communist domination of Eastern Europe, we must realize that it would be impractical to try to free captured peoples. Rather we must use our power to prevent further expansion of the Red Menace."
>
> The analysis above of the situation in Europe after the Second World War provided the rationale for which of the following United States policies?
>
> (A) Flexible response
>
> (B) Massive retaliation
>
> (C) Liberation
>
> (D) Containment

Given the placement of the phrase "which of the following," you can tell that the list of answer choices is a list of "policies." You are supposed to pick the policy that is defended in the analysis given.

Being able to select the right answer depends on your understanding of the analysis given. Try to rephrase the selection in your own words. You might come up with something like "We cannot free the people of Eastern Europe who are dominated by communism, but we can use our power to prevent further domination by communists." This helps lead you to the correct answer, (D). "Containment" is the name given to the policy of trying to "contain" the spread of communism.

Understanding Questions Containing "NOT," "LEAST," "EXCEPT"

In addition to "which of the following" and details that must be understood, the words "NOT," "EXCEPT," and "LEAST" often make comprehension of test questions more difficult. These words are always capitalized when they appear in The Praxis Series test questions, but they are easily (and frequently) overlooked.

For the following test question, determine what kind of answer you're looking for and what the details of the question are.

> The Fair Labor Standards Act of 1938 did all of the following EXCEPT
>
> (A) establish a minimum wage of 40 cents an hour
>
> (B) require the hiring of women and members of minority groups for some government jobs

(C) fix the workweek at 40 hours

(D) forbid the hiring of workers under the age of sixteen

You're looking for the provision that was NOT part of the Fair Labor Standards Act. (B) is the answer — that is, all of the other choices *were* included in the act. (The federal government at that time made little or no effort to promote any kind of quotas to promote hiring of women and members of minority groups.)

TIP It's easy to get confused while you're processing the information to answer a question with a LEAST, NOT, or EXCEPT in the question. If you treat the word "LEAST," "NOT," or "EXCEPT" as one of the details you must satisfy, you have a better chance of understanding what the question is asking. And when you check your answer, make "LEAST," "NOT," or "EXCEPT" one of the details you check for.

Here's an example of a question that uses the word "LEAST."

Which of the following nations is LEAST self-sufficient in the natural resources needed for modern industry?

(A) United States

(B) Japan

(C) France

(D) United Kingdom

You're looking for the nation with the *smallest* amounts of raw materials to support its industrial economy. The answer is (B).

Again, the key to answering questions with LEAST is remembering that you are looking for the *smallest* or *lowest* degree as your correct answer.

For questions with EXCEPT or NOT, you are looking for the *incorrect* choice as your correct answer.

Be Familiar with Multiple-Choice Question Types

You will probably see more than one question format on a multiple-choice test. Here are examples of some of the more common question formats.

1. Complete the statement

In this type of question, you are given an incomplete statement. You must select the choice that will make the completed statement correct.

The emergence in the 1960's of movements such as the Black Muslims and the Black Panthers reflected the

(A) continuing support of Black Americans for the goals of Martin Luther King Jr.

(B) failure of federal legislation to satisfy the rising expectations of Black Americans

(C) renewed dedication among Black Americans to work with White liberals toward achieving equality

(D) growing economic power of young Black Americans

To check your answer, reread the question and add your answer choice at the end. Be sure that your choice best completes the sentence.

The correct answer is (B). Civil rights legislation was slow to address the concerns of Black Americans. The Black Panthers were originally formed to patrol black neighborhoods and to protect residents from what Panthers believed were acts of brutality by police. The Black Muslims aimed to create and legitimate a separate social identity for Blacks outside the predominant culture, which they viewed as the creation of a White racist society.

2. Which of the following

This question type is discussed in detail in a previous section. Also discussed above are strategies for helping you understand what the question is asking and for understanding details in the question that will help you select the correct choice. Consider this additional example.

The climate of Britain is milder than that of most other places along the same latitude for which of the following reasons?

(A) The Gulf Stream brings warm waters to Britain, raising the temperature of winds that blow onto the island.

(B) Hot springs throughout the country raise the temperature of the surrounding land and air.

(C) Mountain ranges in the north of Britain act as a barrier to cold winds blowing from the Arctic.

(D) Small landmasses generate their own local climate and are largely unaffected by latitude.

The question above asks you to choose the reason Britain's climate is comparatively mild for its latitude. (The correct answer is (A).)

3. Roman numeral choices

This format is used when there can be more than one correct answer in the list. Consider the following example.

The term "gender gap" is used in a political science context to refer to differences in survey response data from women and men in which of the following areas?

   I. The relative importance of domestic versus foreign-policy issues

   II. Attitudes regarding such social issues as gun control or pornography

   III. Specific foreign-policy issues, such as military issues

(A) I only

(B) II only

(C) I and III only

(D) I, II, and III

One useful strategy in this type of question is to assess each possible answer before looking at the answer choices. Then evaluate the answer options. In the question above, survey research has typically shown significant differences between men and women in all three of the areas. So the answer is (D).

4. LEAST, EXCEPT, NOT

This question type is discussed at length above. It asks you to select the choice that doesn't fit. You must be very careful with this question type, because it's easy to forget that you're selecting the negative. This question type is used in situations in which there are several good solutions, or ways to approach something, but also a clearly wrong way to do something.

5. Questions about graphs, tables, or reading passages

The important thing to keep in mind when answering questions about tables, graphs, or reading passages is to answer the question that is asked. In the case of a map or graph, you should consider reading the questions first, and then look at the map or graph in light of the questions you have to answer. In the case of a long reading passage, you might want to go ahead and read the passage, marking places you think are important, and then answer the questions.

Look at this example.

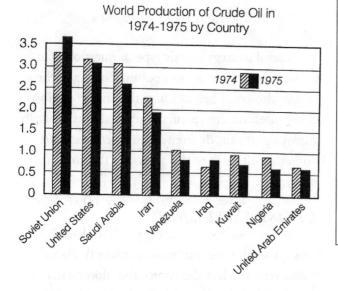

World Production of Crude Oil in 1974-1975 by Country

How many of the countries shown in the graph above produced more crude oil in 1975 than in 1974?

(A) None

(B) One

(C) Two

(D) Three

There is no reason to spend a great deal of time trying to understand the entire graph in detail when you are being asked a very specific question about it. Here the best approach is to read the question and then look at the graph with the question in mind. You can quickly see that two countries produced more crude oil in 1975 than in 1974, so the answer is (C).

Here is another example.

ESTIMATED POPULATION OF AMERICAN COLONIES, 1630 AND 1750		
	1630	**1750**
New England		
White inhabitants	1,796	349,029
Black inhabitants	0	10,982
Middle Colonies		
White inhabitants	340	275,723
Black inhabitants	10	20,736
Southern Colonies		
White inhabitants	2,450	309,588
Black inhabitants	50	204,702
Total		
White inhabitants	4,586	934,340
Black inhabitants	60	236,420

Which of the following is a correct statement supported by the chart above?

(A) Religion was a powerful force opposing slavery in the American colonies.

(B) Slavery grew rapidly throughout the American colonies despite restrictions on the slave trade.

(C) Southern landholders preferred the labor of indentured servants to slave labor.

(D) By 1750, the southern colonies had become demographically distinct from the other colonies.

As with the question about the graph above, the best way to approach this question would be to look at the question before studying the table. You might want to look over the table briefly in order to get yourself oriented. (What is it about? How is it organized?) But the key to answering correctly is reading the question and using the table to answer it.

The only claim that is fully supported by the table is (D). No other answer can be drawn solely from this chart.

6. Other formats

New formats are developed from time to time in order to find new ways of assessing knowledge with multiple-choice questions. If you see a format you are not familiar with, read the directions carefully. Then read and approach the question the way you would any other question, asking yourself what you are supposed to be looking for, and what details are given in the question that help you find the answer.

Useful facts about the test

1. **You can answer the sections of the test in any order.** You can go through the questions from beginning to end, as many test takers do, or you can create your own path. Perhaps you will want to answer questions in your strongest field first and then move from your strengths to your weaker areas. There is no right or wrong way. Use the approach that works for you.

2. **There are no trick questions on the test.** You don't have to find any hidden meanings or worry about trick wording. All of the questions on the test ask about subject matter knowledge in a straightforward manner.

3. **Don't worry about answer patterns.** There is one myth that says that answers on multiple-choice tests follow patterns. There is another myth that there will never be more than two questions with the same lettered answer following each other. There is no truth to either of these myths. Select the answer you think is correct, based on your knowledge of the subject.

4. **There is no penalty for guessing.** Your test score is based on the number of correct answers you have, and incorrect answers are not counted against you. When you don't know the answer to a question, try to eliminate any obviously wrong answers and then guess at the correct one.

5. **It's OK to write in your test booklet.** You can work problems right on the pages of the booklet, make notes to yourself, mark questions you want to review later, or write anything at all. Your test booklet will be destroyed after you are finished with it, so use it in any way that is helpful to you.

Smart tips for taking the test

1. **Put your answers in the right "bubbles."** It seems obvious, but be sure that you are "bubbling in" the answer to the right question on your answer sheet. You would be surprised at how many candidates fill in a "bubble" without checking to see that the number matches the question they are answering.

2. **Skip the questions you find to be extremely difficult.** There are bound to be some questions that you think are hard. Rather than trying to answer these on your first pass through the test, leave them blank and mark them in your test booklet so that you can come back to them.

Pay attention to the time as you answer the rest of the questions on the test and try to finish with 10 or 15 minutes remaining so that you can go back over the questions you left blank. Even if you don't know the answer the second time you read the questions, see if you can narrow down the possible answers, and then guess.

3. **Keep track of the time.** Bring a watch to the test, just in case the clock in the test room is difficult for you to see. Remember that, on average, you have one minute to answer each of the 120 questions. One minute may not seem like much time, but you will be able to answer a number of questions in only a few seconds each. You will probably have plenty of time to answer all of the questions, but if you find yourself becoming bogged down in one section, you might decide to move on and come back to that section later.

4. **Read all of the possible answers before selecting one**—and then reread the question to be sure the answer you have selected really answers the question being asked. Remember that a question that contains a phrase like "Which of the following does NOT . . ." is asking for the one answer that is NOT a correct statement or conclusion.

5. **Check your answers.** If you have extra time left over at the end of the test, look over each question and make sure that you have filled in the "bubble" on the answer sheet as you intended. Many candidates make careless mistakes that could have been corrected if they had checked their answers.

6. **Don't worry about your score when you are taking the test.** No one is expected to get all of the questions correct. Your score on this test is not analogous to your score on the SAT, the GRE, or other similar tests. It doesn't matter on this test whether you score very high or barely pass. If you meet the minimum passing scores for your state, and you meet the other requirements of the state for obtaining a teaching license, you will receive a license. Your actual score doesn't matter, as long as it is above the minimum required score. With your score report you will receive a booklet entitled *Understanding Your Praxis Scores,* which lists the passing scores for your state.

Chapter 11
Practice Questions

▶   ▶   ▶   ▶   ▶   ▶   ▶   ▶   ▶   ▶   ▶   ▶

Practice Questions

Now that you have studied the content topics in the six areas and have worked through strategies relating to multiple-choice questions, you should take the following practice questions. You will probably find it helpful to simulate actual testing conditions, giving yourself about 110 minutes to work on the questions. You can cut out and use the answer sheet provided if you wish.

Keep in mind that the test you take at an actual administration will have different questions, although the proportion of questions in each area and major subarea will be approximately the same. You should not expect the percentage of questions you answer correctly in these practice questions to be exactly the same as when you take the test at an actual administration, since numerous factors affect a person's performance in any given testing situation.

When you have finished the practice questions, you can score your answers and read the explanations of the best answer choices in chapter 12.

Social Studies:
Content Knowledge

Practice Questions

Time—110 Minutes

117 Questions

(Note, at the official test administration of the *Social Studies: Content Knowledge* test, there will be 130 questions, and you will be allowed 120 minutes to complete the test. At the official test administration of the *Citizenship Education: Content Knowledge* test, there will be 115 questions, and you will be allowed 120 minutes to complete the test.)

DO NOT USE INK

1. NAME

Enter your last name and first initial.
Omit spaces, hyphens, apostrophes, etc.

Last Name
(first 6 letters) | F I

(A) (B) (C) (D) (E) (F) (G) (H) (I) (J) (K) (L) (M) (N) (O) (P) (Q) (R) (S) (T) (U) (V) (W) (X) (Y) (Z)

Use only a pencil with soft black lead (No. 2 or HB) to complete this answer sheet.
Be sure to fill in completely the oval that corresponds to the proper letter or number.
Completely erase any errors or stray marks.

2.

YOUR NAME: (Print)
Last Name (Family or Surname) — First Name (Given) — M. I.

MAILING ADDRESS: (Print)
P.O. Box or Street Address

Apt. # (If any)

City — State or Province

Country — Zip or Postal Code

TELEPHONE NUMBER: ( ) Home — ( ) Business

SIGNATURE: _____ **TEST DATE:** _____

PRAXIS
THE PRAXIS SERIES
Professional Assessments for Beginning Teachers®

Answer Sheet C

PAGE 1

3. DATE OF BIRTH

Month	Day
Jan.	
Feb.	
Mar.	
April	
May	
June	
July	
Aug.	
Sept.	
Oct.	
Nov.	
Dec.	

4. SOCIAL SECURITY NUMBER

(0) (1) (2) (3) (4) (5) (6) (7) (8) (9)

5. CANDIDATE ID NUMBER

(0) (1) (2) (3) (4) (5) (6) (7) (8) (9)

6. TEST CENTER / REPORTING LOCATION

Center Number — Room Number

Center Name

City — State or Province

Country

7. TEST CODE / FORM CODE

(0) (1) (2) (3) (4) (5) (6) (7) (8) (9)

0
1

8. TEST BOOK SERIAL NUMBER

9. TEST FORM

10. TEST NAME

Educational Testing Service, ETS, the ETS logo, and THE PRAXIS SERIES:PROFESSIONAL ASSESSMENTS FOR BEGINNING TEACHERS and its logo are registered trademarks of Educational Testing Service.

(ETS) Educational Testing Service

51055 • 08920 • TF71M500   Q2573-06
MH01159

I.N. 202974

1   2   3   4

CERTIFICATION STATEMENT: (Please write the following statement below. DO NOT PRINT.)

"I hereby agree to the conditions set forth in the *Registration Bulletin* and certify that I am the person whose name and address appear on this answer sheet."

_____

_____

_____

SIGNATURE: _____ DATE: _____ / _____ / _____

Month   Day   Year

BE SURE EACH MARK IS DARK AND COMPLETELY FILLS THE INTENDED SPACE AS ILLUSTRATED HERE: ●

1 Ⓐ Ⓑ Ⓒ Ⓓ	41 Ⓐ Ⓑ Ⓒ Ⓓ	81 Ⓐ Ⓑ Ⓒ Ⓓ	121 Ⓐ Ⓑ Ⓒ Ⓓ
2 Ⓐ Ⓑ Ⓒ Ⓓ	42 Ⓐ Ⓑ Ⓒ Ⓓ	82 Ⓐ Ⓑ Ⓒ Ⓓ	122 Ⓐ Ⓑ Ⓒ Ⓓ
3 Ⓐ Ⓑ Ⓒ Ⓓ	43 Ⓐ Ⓑ Ⓒ Ⓓ	83 Ⓐ Ⓑ Ⓒ Ⓓ	123 Ⓐ Ⓑ Ⓒ Ⓓ
4 Ⓐ Ⓑ Ⓒ Ⓓ	44 Ⓐ Ⓑ Ⓒ Ⓓ	84 Ⓐ Ⓑ Ⓒ Ⓓ	124 Ⓐ Ⓑ Ⓒ Ⓓ
5 Ⓐ Ⓑ Ⓒ Ⓓ	45 Ⓐ Ⓑ Ⓒ Ⓓ	85 Ⓐ Ⓑ Ⓒ Ⓓ	125 Ⓐ Ⓑ Ⓒ Ⓓ
6 Ⓐ Ⓑ Ⓒ Ⓓ	46 Ⓐ Ⓑ Ⓒ Ⓓ	86 Ⓐ Ⓑ Ⓒ Ⓓ	126 Ⓐ Ⓑ Ⓒ Ⓓ
7 Ⓐ Ⓑ Ⓒ Ⓓ	47 Ⓐ Ⓑ Ⓒ Ⓓ	87 Ⓐ Ⓑ Ⓒ Ⓓ	127 Ⓐ Ⓑ Ⓒ Ⓓ
8 Ⓐ Ⓑ Ⓒ Ⓓ	48 Ⓐ Ⓑ Ⓒ Ⓓ	88 Ⓐ Ⓑ Ⓒ Ⓓ	128 Ⓐ Ⓑ Ⓒ Ⓓ
9 Ⓐ Ⓑ Ⓒ Ⓓ	49 Ⓐ Ⓑ Ⓒ Ⓓ	89 Ⓐ Ⓑ Ⓒ Ⓓ	129 Ⓐ Ⓑ Ⓒ Ⓓ
10 Ⓐ Ⓑ Ⓒ Ⓓ	50 Ⓐ Ⓑ Ⓒ Ⓓ	90 Ⓐ Ⓑ Ⓒ Ⓓ	130 Ⓐ Ⓑ Ⓒ Ⓓ
11 Ⓐ Ⓑ Ⓒ Ⓓ	51 Ⓐ Ⓑ Ⓒ Ⓓ	91 Ⓐ Ⓑ Ⓒ Ⓓ	131 Ⓐ Ⓑ Ⓒ Ⓓ
12 Ⓐ Ⓑ Ⓒ Ⓓ	52 Ⓐ Ⓑ Ⓒ Ⓓ	92 Ⓐ Ⓑ Ⓒ Ⓓ	132 Ⓐ Ⓑ Ⓒ Ⓓ
13 Ⓐ Ⓑ Ⓒ Ⓓ	53 Ⓐ Ⓑ Ⓒ Ⓓ	93 Ⓐ Ⓑ Ⓒ Ⓓ	133 Ⓐ Ⓑ Ⓒ Ⓓ
14 Ⓐ Ⓑ Ⓒ Ⓓ	54 Ⓐ Ⓑ Ⓒ Ⓓ	94 Ⓐ Ⓑ Ⓒ Ⓓ	134 Ⓐ Ⓑ Ⓒ Ⓓ
15 Ⓐ Ⓑ Ⓒ Ⓓ	55 Ⓐ Ⓑ Ⓒ Ⓓ	95 Ⓐ Ⓑ Ⓒ Ⓓ	135 Ⓐ Ⓑ Ⓒ Ⓓ
16 Ⓐ Ⓑ Ⓒ Ⓓ	56 Ⓐ Ⓑ Ⓒ Ⓓ	96 Ⓐ Ⓑ Ⓒ Ⓓ	136 Ⓐ Ⓑ Ⓒ Ⓓ
17 Ⓐ Ⓑ Ⓒ Ⓓ	57 Ⓐ Ⓑ Ⓒ Ⓓ	97 Ⓐ Ⓑ Ⓒ Ⓓ	137 Ⓐ Ⓑ Ⓒ Ⓓ
18 Ⓐ Ⓑ Ⓒ Ⓓ	58 Ⓐ Ⓑ Ⓒ Ⓓ	98 Ⓐ Ⓑ Ⓒ Ⓓ	138 Ⓐ Ⓑ Ⓒ Ⓓ
19 Ⓐ Ⓑ Ⓒ Ⓓ	59 Ⓐ Ⓑ Ⓒ Ⓓ	99 Ⓐ Ⓑ Ⓒ Ⓓ	139 Ⓐ Ⓑ Ⓒ Ⓓ
20 Ⓐ Ⓑ Ⓒ Ⓓ	60 Ⓐ Ⓑ Ⓒ Ⓓ	100 Ⓐ Ⓑ Ⓒ Ⓓ	140 Ⓐ Ⓑ Ⓒ Ⓓ
21 Ⓐ Ⓑ Ⓒ Ⓓ	61 Ⓐ Ⓑ Ⓒ Ⓓ	101 Ⓐ Ⓑ Ⓒ Ⓓ	141 Ⓐ Ⓑ Ⓒ Ⓓ
22 Ⓐ Ⓑ Ⓒ Ⓓ	62 Ⓐ Ⓑ Ⓒ Ⓓ	102 Ⓐ Ⓑ Ⓒ Ⓓ	142 Ⓐ Ⓑ Ⓒ Ⓓ
23 Ⓐ Ⓑ Ⓒ Ⓓ	63 Ⓐ Ⓑ Ⓒ Ⓓ	103 Ⓐ Ⓑ Ⓒ Ⓓ	143 Ⓐ Ⓑ Ⓒ Ⓓ
24 Ⓐ Ⓑ Ⓒ Ⓓ	64 Ⓐ Ⓑ Ⓒ Ⓓ	104 Ⓐ Ⓑ Ⓒ Ⓓ	144 Ⓐ Ⓑ Ⓒ Ⓓ
25 Ⓐ Ⓑ Ⓒ Ⓓ	65 Ⓐ Ⓑ Ⓒ Ⓓ	105 Ⓐ Ⓑ Ⓒ Ⓓ	145 Ⓐ Ⓑ Ⓒ Ⓓ
26 Ⓐ Ⓑ Ⓒ Ⓓ	66 Ⓐ Ⓑ Ⓒ Ⓓ	106 Ⓐ Ⓑ Ⓒ Ⓓ	146 Ⓐ Ⓑ Ⓒ Ⓓ
27 Ⓐ Ⓑ Ⓒ Ⓓ	67 Ⓐ Ⓑ Ⓒ Ⓓ	107 Ⓐ Ⓑ Ⓒ Ⓓ	147 Ⓐ Ⓑ Ⓒ Ⓓ
28 Ⓐ Ⓑ Ⓒ Ⓓ	68 Ⓐ Ⓑ Ⓒ Ⓓ	108 Ⓐ Ⓑ Ⓒ Ⓓ	148 Ⓐ Ⓑ Ⓒ Ⓓ
29 Ⓐ Ⓑ Ⓒ Ⓓ	69 Ⓐ Ⓑ Ⓒ Ⓓ	109 Ⓐ Ⓑ Ⓒ Ⓓ	149 Ⓐ Ⓑ Ⓒ Ⓓ
30 Ⓐ Ⓑ Ⓒ Ⓓ	70 Ⓐ Ⓑ Ⓒ Ⓓ	110 Ⓐ Ⓑ Ⓒ Ⓓ	150 Ⓐ Ⓑ Ⓒ Ⓓ
31 Ⓐ Ⓑ Ⓒ Ⓓ	71 Ⓐ Ⓑ Ⓒ Ⓓ	111 Ⓐ Ⓑ Ⓒ Ⓓ	151 Ⓐ Ⓑ Ⓒ Ⓓ
32 Ⓐ Ⓑ Ⓒ Ⓓ	72 Ⓐ Ⓑ Ⓒ Ⓓ	112 Ⓐ Ⓑ Ⓒ Ⓓ	152 Ⓐ Ⓑ Ⓒ Ⓓ
33 Ⓐ Ⓑ Ⓒ Ⓓ	73 Ⓐ Ⓑ Ⓒ Ⓓ	113 Ⓐ Ⓑ Ⓒ Ⓓ	153 Ⓐ Ⓑ Ⓒ Ⓓ
34 Ⓐ Ⓑ Ⓒ Ⓓ	74 Ⓐ Ⓑ Ⓒ Ⓓ	114 Ⓐ Ⓑ Ⓒ Ⓓ	154 Ⓐ Ⓑ Ⓒ Ⓓ
35 Ⓐ Ⓑ Ⓒ Ⓓ	75 Ⓐ Ⓑ Ⓒ Ⓓ	115 Ⓐ Ⓑ Ⓒ Ⓓ	155 Ⓐ Ⓑ Ⓒ Ⓓ
36 Ⓐ Ⓑ Ⓒ Ⓓ	76 Ⓐ Ⓑ Ⓒ Ⓓ	116 Ⓐ Ⓑ Ⓒ Ⓓ	156 Ⓐ Ⓑ Ⓒ Ⓓ
37 Ⓐ Ⓑ Ⓒ Ⓓ	77 Ⓐ Ⓑ Ⓒ Ⓓ	117 Ⓐ Ⓑ Ⓒ Ⓓ	157 Ⓐ Ⓑ Ⓒ Ⓓ
38 Ⓐ Ⓑ Ⓒ Ⓓ	78 Ⓐ Ⓑ Ⓒ Ⓓ	118 Ⓐ Ⓑ Ⓒ Ⓓ	158 Ⓐ Ⓑ Ⓒ Ⓓ
39 Ⓐ Ⓑ Ⓒ Ⓓ	79 Ⓐ Ⓑ Ⓒ Ⓓ	119 Ⓐ Ⓑ Ⓒ Ⓓ	159 Ⓐ Ⓑ Ⓒ Ⓓ
40 Ⓐ Ⓑ Ⓒ Ⓓ	80 Ⓐ Ⓑ Ⓒ Ⓓ	120 Ⓐ Ⓑ Ⓒ Ⓓ	160 Ⓐ Ⓑ Ⓒ Ⓓ

UNITED STATES HISTORY

1. In which of the following regions of the United States is a farmer most likely to need irrigation to grow crops?

    (A) New England
    (B) Southeast
    (C) Pacific Northwest
    (D) Southwest

2. All of the following states are adjacent to at least one of the Great Lakes EXCEPT

    (A) Michigan
    (B) Iowa
    (C) New York
    (D) Pennsylvania

3. Which of the following climate systems characterizes the southeastern United States?

    (A) Humid subtropical
    (B) Mediterranean
    (C) Tropical savanna
    (D) Desert

4. Which of the following was the principal cause of Iroquois grievances against the British colonies in the early 1750's?

    (A) The Iroquois' role as a trading partner was eroding as British and French colonists increasingly established direct trade relations with each other.
    (B) Pennsylvania was encouraging tribes in its western districts to move north into Iroquois territory.
    (C) Colonial westward expansion brought increasing numbers of settlers and troops onto Iroquois land.
    (D) The British government failed to pay the Iroquois for their assistance during the French and Indian War.

5. Which of the following Native American tribes was forced off its land by the Indian Removal Act of 1830 and resettled in the Indian Territory?

    (A) Iroquois
    (B) Cherokee
    (C) Pueblo
    (D) Sioux

6. In the early years of European exploration and settlement of North America, the Native American population changed in which of the following ways?

    (A) It grew, largely as a result of the spread of European crops.
    (B) It decreased, largely as a result of European military attacks.
    (C) It decreased, largely as a result of changes in the climate.
    (D) It decreased, largely as result of the spread of infectious diseases from Europeans.

7. "That world of misery, that lake of burning brimstone, is extended abroad under you. There is the dreadful pit of the glowing flames of the wrath of God; there is hell's wide gaping mouth open; and you have nothing to stand upon, nor anything to take hold of; there is nothing between you and hell but the air; it is only the power and mere pleasure of God that holds you up."

    The quote above is most closely associated with what social movement?

    (A) First Great Awakening
    (B) Emancipation movement
    (C) Utopianism
    (D) Temperance movement

8. The arrangement of political institutions chosen by the framers of the Constitution was most closely modeled on which of the following governments?

    (A) The Indian Confederations
    (B) The democracy of ancient Athens
    (C) The ancient Roman republic
    (D) The British Parliamentary system

9. A major weakness of the national government under the Articles of Confederation was its inability to

    (A) print money
    (B) levy taxes
    (C) declare war
    (D) conduct foreign diplomacy

10. ". . . slavery is inconsistent with the genius of republicanism, and has a tendency to destroy those principles on which it is supported, as it lessens the sense of the equal rights of mankind, and habituates us to tyranny and oppression."

    Which of the following best reflects the sentiment of the author of the quote above?

    (A) Slavery can erode the ideals of a republic.
    (B) Slavery is an ineffective economic practice.
    (C) In a republic slavery will die out if left alone.
    (D) Slavery is not a political issue in a republic.

11. "Those who labour in the earth are the chosen people of God, if ever he had a chosen people, whose breasts he has made his peculiar deposit for substantial and genuine virtue."

    This passage is consistent with the political ideology of which of the following historical figures?

    (A) Alexander Hamilton
    (B) John Adams
    (C) John Marshall
    (D) Thomas Jefferson

12. Which of the following mid-nineteenth-century reform movements had the most difficulty gaining adherents and influencing society?

    (A) Temperance
    (B) Public education
    (C) Women's rights
    (D) Abolition

Question 13 is based on the following painting.

Museum of the City of New York.
Harry T. Peters Collection (56.300.107).
Photograph © Museum of the City of New York.

13. The painting above captures the spirit of which political ideology?

    (A) Manifest destiny
    (B) Social Darwinism
    (C) Imperialism
    (D) Progressivism

14. "In all social systems there must be a class to do the menial duties, to perform the drudgery of life. That is, a class requiring but a low order of intellect and but little skill. Its requisites are vigor, docility, fidelity. Such a class you must have, or you would not have that other class which leads progress, civilization, and refinement."

What is the essence of James H. Hammond's argument as set forth in the statement above?

(A) Conflict between the "haves" and the "have-nots" in society is inevitable.
(B) The United States must expand beyond its borders to guarantee a supply of menial labor.
(C) Slavery is not an optional but a necessary component of an advanced society.
(D) Industrialization requires the development of a permanent working class.

15. Which of the following novels had the greatest impact on the abolitionist movement?

(A) *Native Son*
(B) *Uncle Tom's Cabin*
(C) *Huckleberry Finn*
(D) *Gone with the Wind*

Question 16 is based on the following cartoon.

Reprinted by permission of
The New York Public Library

16. The concerns expressed in this 1872 political cartoon eventually led to the passage of legislation establishing

(A) a government civil service
(B) expanded rights for women
(C) a federal sanitation code
(D) restrictions on political reporting

17. "The 'sweater' is only possible under a competitive system of industry. He is the natural outcome of cupidity and the intense desire for large profits and quick returns on the one side and the want, misery, degradation and ignorance of the workers on the other . . . These 'sweater's' dens are always located in the most wretched, over-crowded tenement house districts."

Which of the following measures would the speaker quoted above most likely advocate?

(A) Adherence to the gold standard
(B) Lower tariffs
(C) An eight-hour workday
(D) Relocation of clothing factories to other countries

18. Once in khaki suits,
Gee we looked swell,
Full of that Yankee Doodle-de-dum.
Half a million boots sloggin' through Hell,
I was the kid with the drum.
Say, don't you remember, they called me Al—
It was Al all the time.
Say, don't you remember I'm your pal—
Brother can you spare a dime?

The narrator of this song was most likely a veteran of the

(A) Civil War
(B) First World War
(C) Second World War
(D) Korean War

19. What legal doctrine was overturned in the Supreme Court's *Brown* v. *Board of Education* decision in 1954 ?

(A) Universal schooling
(B) "Separate but equal" laws
(C) Prayer in school
(D) Sanctity of the flag

20. "Communists have infiltrated into the school system. We know that teachers in Harvard are avowed Communists. They are spreading Communism in every way they can."

Which political figure came to prominence espousing the sentiments expressed in this quote?

(A) Adlai Stevenson
(B) Harry Truman
(C) Joseph McCarthy
(D) Dwight Eisenhower

21. "The short-run effects should be very favorable to the United States. Unquestionably, the United States will emerge from this confrontation with increased prestige worldwide. The Soviet action should demonstrate once again the offensive nature of Soviet motivations more clearly than anything we could say. It should also demonstrate that the Soviets are not prepared to risk a decisive military showdown with the United States over issues involving the extension of Soviet power."

This passage was most likely written in the aftermath of which of the following conflicts?

(A) Cuban missile crisis
(B) Vietnam War
(C) Invasion of Afghanistan
(D) Korean War

Question 22 is based on the following graphs.

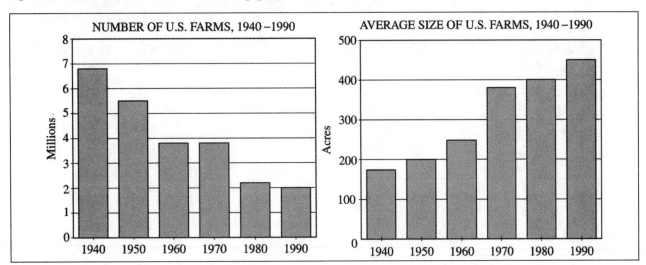

22. Which of the following developments contributed to the trends shown in the graphs above?

   (A) Increasing federal subsidies to support family farms
   (B) Decreasing rainfall across the United States
   (C) Increasing prices for United States agricultural products
   (D) Increasing mechanization of agriculture

23. Which of the following civil rights activists is most closely associated with the Montgomery bus boycott?

   (A) Ella Baker
   (B) Angela Davis
   (C) Martin Luther King Jr.
   (D) Malcolm X

WORLD HISTORY

24. Among scholars there is general agreement that humanity's immediate ancestor, *Homo erectus,* first developed in

    (A) Africa
    (B) Australia
    (C) East Asia
    (D) Europe

Question 25 is based on the following painting.

Douglas Mazonowicz
Art Resource, NY

25. Works such as the one shown above are most closely associated with which of following types of societies?

    (A) Settled agricultural
    (B) Slash-and-burn agricultural
    (C) Nomadic herding
    (D) Hunting and gathering

26. "This ancient civilization possessed a highly organized system of government, had a polytheistic religion for most of its history, controlled crop production through a sophisticated form of irrigation, and created a unique form of pictorial writing."

The quotation above describes which of the following ancient civilizations?

(A) Aryan
(B) Greek
(C) Egyptian
(D) Mongol

Question 27 is based on the following map.

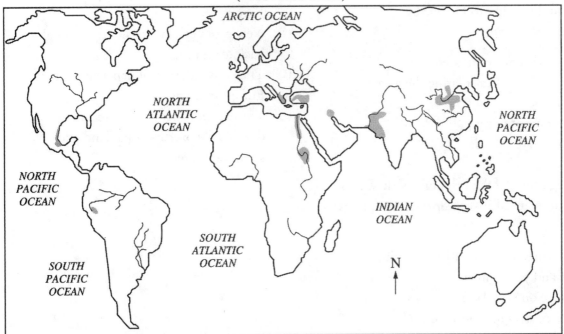

EARLY CIVILIZATIONS
(3500–1000 B.C.E.)

27. In the map above, gray regions represent the locations of early civilizations. Which of the following can be concluded about early civilizations from the map?

(A) They tended to form in river valleys and along coasts.
(B) They tended to form in tropical regions.
(C) They were often at war with one another over land disputes.
(D) They depended on trade by sea.

28. First Truth: Life is suffering.
Second Truth: Suffering comes from desire.
Third Truth: Curbing desire eliminates suffering.
Fourth Truth: Desire may be eliminated and enlightenment achieved by following the Eightfold Path.

The principles above are basic to which of the following religions?

(A) Hinduism
(B) Buddhism
(C) Islam
(D) Zoroastrianism

29. Which of the following was developed in India and brought to Europe by Arab mathematicians?

(A) The Pythagorean theorem
(B) The method of calculating the area of a circle
(C) The concept of zero
(D) An accurate calendar

30. At the beginning of the Peloponnesian War, a striking difference between Sparta and Athens was Sparta's

(A) regimented and militaristic training of boys and young men
(B) reliance on slave labor
(C) more democratic constitution
(D) refusal to establish colonies

31. All of the following are characteristics of the Roman Empire after it was reorganized by Augustus EXCEPT

(A) increased trade that spanned most of Europe, North Africa, and Asia
(B) the standardization of Roman law throughout empire
(C) the abolition of slavery
(D) overcrowding, pollution, and crime in Rome

32. Which of the following represents a significant result of the European participation in the Crusades?

(A) The strengthening of the Byzantine Empire
(B) New products and knowledge brought back to Europe
(C) The consolidation of papal control over European kings
(D) The establishment of European dominance over Eurasian land and sea trade routes

Question 33 is based on the following map.

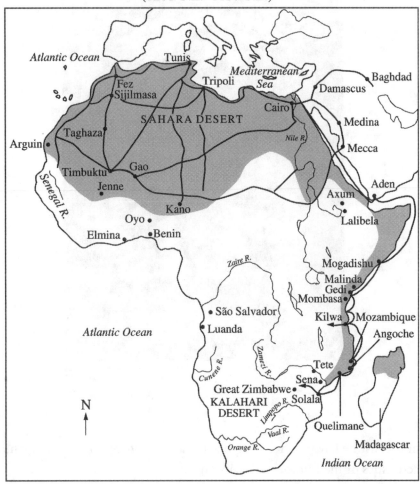

AFRICA
(1200 C.E.–1600 C.E.)

33. The shaded regions and thick solid lines in the map above illustrate which of the following?

(A) The relation between the spread of Islam and the location of major trade routes

(B) The conquest of Africa by European military forces and the major military routes

(C) The relation between the spread of European culture and the routes of European explorers

(D) The region of political unification among major African civilizations after the flourishing of trade

34. Which of the following socioeconomic patterns predominated in both Europe and Japan during the period between 700 and 1300 C.E.?

(A) Urbanization
(B) Feudalism
(C) Capitalism
(D) Guild system

Question 35 is based on the following painting.

Alinari
Art Resource, NY

35. This painting in the Sistine Chapel, from Michelangelo's *Last Judgment,* reflects which of the following characteristics of the European Renaissance?

(A) The increasing emphasis on the consequences of religious obedience
(B) The triumph of mysticism over reason in the Roman Catholic church
(C) The expression of religious sentiment through glorification of human achievement
(D) The mutual influence of Roman Catholic values and those of the invading Ottoman Empire

<u>Question 36</u> is based on the following painting.

Tokyo National Museum

36. This Japanese painting from the sixteenth century exemplifies which of the following views of nature?

(A) Nature operates according to rules that humans can discover and use.

(B) Nature is very powerful, and human control of nature is very limited.

(C) Nature is brutal, and humans should avoid contact with nature.

(D) Nature symbolizes the joy that humans should show toward all aspects of life.

37. All of the following were reactions of the Catholic Church to the Protestant Reformation EXCEPT

(A) the Inquisition
(B) censorship
(C) funding of the arts and Baroque architecture
(D) translation of the Bible into vernacular languages

38. "From the day the nation . . . allowed kings to establish a general tax without its consent, and the nobility had the cowardice to let the third estate be taxed, provided that the nobility itself remained exempt; from that day the seed was sown of nearly all the vices and abuses which the old regime practiced for the rest of its life, vices and abuses which ended by bringing about the violent death of the old regime."—*Alexis de Tocqueville*

According to Tocqueville, which of the following was a root cause of the French Revolution?

(A) The rise of a middle class that was exempt from taxation
(B) Discriminatory taxation against the poorer classes
(C) The use of taxes to support military repression
(D) A weak bureaucratic structure funded by increased taxes

39. "Early next day we left Iztapalapa with a large escort of these great *caciques*,[1] and followed the causeway, which is eight yards wide and goes so straight to the city of Mexico that I do not think it curves at all. Wide though it was, it was so crowded with people that there was hardly room for them all. Some were going to Mexico and others coming away, besides those who had come out to see us, and we could hardly get through the crowds that were there. For the towers were full, and they came in canoes from all parts of the lake. No wonder, since they had never seen horses or men like us before!"

[1] *native Indian chiefs*

Which of the following is the most likely author of the quotation above?

(A) A soldier in the Cortés expedition that conquered the Aztec Empire
(B) Pachacuti, the ruler of the Inca Empire
(C) Magellan as he was searching for the way around the Americas
(D) A crew member on Christopher Columbus' first voyage to the New World

40. "Our epoch, the epoch of the bourgeoisie, possesses, however, this distinctive feature: it has simplified the class antagonisms. Society as a whole is more and more splitting up into two great hostile camps, into two great classes directly facing each other: bourgeoisie and proletariat."

The quotation above expresses one of the major tenets of which of the following?

(A) Utopian socialism
(B) Marxism
(C) Laissez-faire economics
(D) Social Darwinism

Question 41 is based on the cartoon and the quotation below.

"A lady, to be such, must be a mere lady. She must not work for profit,
or engage in any occupation that money can command."
—*Englishwoman Margaretta Greg,* 1853

41. Which of the following statements about women in Victorian England is best supported by the cartoon (from the 1840's) and the quotation above?

   (A) Modern technology was gradually causing conditions to improve for women.

   (B) Women in Victorian England had more opportunities for education and entry into the workforce than did women in other European countries.

   (C) Working conditions for women in the laboring class contrasted sharply with Victorian ideals of womanhood.

   (D) Women in the lower class expected to gain social and economic benefits through the political activities of upper- and middle-class women.

Question 42 is based on the following cartoon.

THE GAME OF THE DAY.

BISMARCK. "COME, ANDRASSY, WE KNOW EACH OTHER'S 'FORM.' YOU AND I TOGETHER AGAINST THE LOT!!"
RUSSIA (to FRANCE). "I THINK, MADAME, *WE* MIGHT BE A MATCH FOR THEM!"
FRANCE. "THANKS! I PREFER TO SIT OUT AT PRESENT!"   ENGLAND (to ITALY). "NOBODY ASKS *US!!*"

42. Which of the following political developments is depicted in the 1879 cartoon above?

(A) The rise of socialist political organizations
(B) Isolationist policies of European nations
(C) The creation of the League of Nations
(D) The creation of alliance systems among European powers

43. "This 'Long March' took people 6,000 miles in one year, 17 miles a day over desolate mountains and through swamps and deserts, pursued by the army and bombed by aircraft. Of the 100,000 Chinese who left Southeast China, only 4,000 reached Shanxi (near the China's northwest border) a year later. The government thought that it was finally rid of the Communists."

The quotation above describes which of the following events?

(A) The Japanese military invasion of China in the 1930's
(B) The forced relocation of peasants to industrial areas during the Cultural Revolution
(C) The retreat by Chinese Communist forces to northwestern China in 1937
(D) The exodus of Chinese Nationalists to Taiwan in 1949

Question 44 is based on the following cartoon.

1941

THE ROAD TO THE EAST
from *Herblock: A Cartoonist's Life* (Times Books, 1998)

44. Which of the following best expresses the main point of this political cartoon?

(A) Hitler's German armies were the best organized and most ruthless in the history of Europe.
(B) European nations adopted policies of conciliation and peace toward Hitler's Germany.
(C) Hitler's invasion exposed the French military as little more than a fraudulent myth.
(D) Hitler's invasion of Russia repeated the mistakes of Napoleon's invasion of Russia.

45. Which of the following political leaders modeled his approach for orchestrating social change on Mohandas Gandhi's strategy of peaceful revolution?

    (A) Martin Luther King Jr.
    (B) John F. Kennedy
    (C) Malcolm X
    (D) Franklin Delano Roosevelt

46. Which of the following best describes the nature of conflict and conflict resolution in the last two decades of the twentieth century?

    (A) The forces of ideology and nationalism weakened, so that conflict became extremely rare and almost all disputes were resolved through negotiation.
    (B) Economic unions eliminated trade barriers for most of the world and reduced the gap between rich nations and poor nations, thus eliminating the economic causes of conflicts.
    (C) The United States and Russia created a joint military force that acted quickly to keep conflicts from spreading beyond a single nation or region.
    (D) International intervention and/or sanctions were often used to resolve conflicts or to keep them localized.

GOVERNMENT AND CIVICS

47. Which of the following contemporary political ideologies most strongly supports government protection of individual freedoms?

    (A) Conservatism
    (B) Liberalism
    (C) Socialism
    (D) Nationalism

48. "All history has been a history of class struggles, of struggles between exploited and exploiting, between dominated and dominating classes at various stages of social development; this struggle, however, has now reached a stage where the exploited and oppressed class (the proletariat) can no longer emancipate itself from the class which exploits and oppresses it (the bourgeoisie), without at the same time forever freeing the whole of society from exploitation, oppression, and class struggles."

    The passage above captures a central tenet of which of the following theories?

    (A) Fascism
    (B) Libertarianism
    (C) Capitalism
    (D) Communism

49. Which of the following was the first to establish a theoretical justification for the belief that the legitimacy of a government is based on the consent of the governed?

    (A) Thomas Hobbes' *Leviathan*
    (B) V. I. Lenin's *What Is to Be Done?*
    (C) John Locke's *The Second Treatise of Government*
    (D) Adam Smith's *Wealth of Nations*

50. The political legitimacy of a democratic national government would be most challenged by which of the following?

    (A) Low approval ratings in national public opinion polls
    (B) A close election for the office of chief executive
    (C) Court decisions that overturn national legislation
    (D) A subnational government's refusal to obey a national law

51. Although Thomas Hobbes and John Locke both presented views of government as a social contract between people and rulers, their views differed in that Hobbes argued that

   (A) people are born free, whereas Locke argued that people are born in social servitude

   (B) people give up their rights and liberties in exchange for protection by government, whereas Locke argued that government exists to protect those rights and liberties

   (C) government only serves to reinforce class conflict, whereas Locke argued that government serves to protect the economically disadvantaged

   (D) government should provide every citizen with economic equality, whereas Locke argued that government should be limited to providing for national defense

52. Federalism is best defined as a system of government in which

   (A) power is shared by national and subnational governments

   (B) power is centralized in a national government that can delegate certain authority and responsibility to subnational governments

   (C) a group of sovereign governments shares a supranational judicial institution

   (D) citizens determine national policy by voting directly in national referenda

53. Which of the following is a primary function of interest groups in the United States?

   (A) Nominating candidates for state and federal elections

   (B) Providing legislators with specialized information on policy issues

   (C) Raising money to support party-building activities

   (D) Enforcing government regulations in their respective policy areas

54. "No United States President was elected as a third-party candidate in the twentieth century. Therefore, the third-party system has had no effect on American politics."

   Which of the following statements is an accurate claim about third-party candidacies that disputes this statement?

   (A) Third-party candidates are usually members of ethnic minority groups.

   (B) Third-party candidates tend to reduce the total amount of media coverage in an election.

   (C) Third-party candidates often lead to voter confusion, reducing total voter turnout.

   (D) Third-party candidates sometimes force platform shifts in the dominant parties.

55. Which of the following is a power granted exclusively to the President by the United States Constitution?

   (A) Declaring war

   (B) Declaring laws unconstitutional

   (C) Granting pardons

   (D) Ratifying treaties

56. The Bill of Rights was added to the United States Constitution explicitly to ensure protection from abuse of power by

    (A) the national government
    (B) political majorities
    (C) individual citizens
    (D) religious institutions

57. Which of the following age-groups has had the lowest voter turnout in the most recent United States elections?

    (A) 18–24
    (B) 25–36
    (C) 37–50
    (D) 51 and older

58. Compared to that of most other developed democracies, voter turnout in the United States in the last several decades has been

    (A) about the same
    (B) slightly higher
    (C) much higher
    (D) significantly lower

59. Which of the following accurately describes a significant difference between the House of Representatives and the Senate?

    (A) Only the Senate can introduce revenue bills.
    (B) Only the Senate allows unlimited debate on all bills.
    (C) Senate representation is based on single-member districts, whereas the House is based on proportional representation.
    (D) In the House, states are represented equally, whereas in the Senate, representation is determined by state population.

60. Which of the following is an example of the legislative oversight function of Congress?

    (A) The Senate rejects the President's proposed budget.
    (B) A supermajority in Congress overrides a presidential veto.
    (C) Congress adopts a new bill requiring states to regulate levels of contaminants in drinking water.
    (D) The Agriculture committee holds hearings about the work of the Environmental Protection Agency.

61. In general, which of the following best describes a difference between federal block grants and federal categorical grants?

    (A) Block grants are used to fund state programs, whereas categorical grants are used to fund federal programs.
    (B) Block grants typically require matching funds from a local government, whereas categorical grants do not.
    (C) Categorical grants have more restrictions than do block grants on how the federal money may be used.
    (D) Categorical grants are given to all states, whereas block grants are given only on a state-by-state basis.

62. "The United States should keep its troops at home. So many ethnic battles are occurring at any one time throughout the world that it is impossible for the United States to act as the world's police officer. We pay good money to the United Nations—let its troops solve the world's minor ethnic flare-ups."

The quotation above most closely resembles which of the following policy approaches?

(A) Imperialism
(B) Internationalism
(C) Interventionism
(D) Isolationism

63. A "direct democracy" exists when citizens do which of the following?

(A) Participate without intermediaries in government decision-making
(B) Elect representatives to participate in government decision-making
(C) Directly elect a chief executive who decides on the enactment of laws
(D) Vote to approve or overturn laws passed by elected representatives

64. During the 1990's in many European countries, right-wing political parties grew more popular in reaction to

(A) trade imbalances between western and eastern Europe
(B) the electoral dominance of socialist political parties
(C) the weakening of the United Nations
(D) the increase in the number of immigrant workers

65. Which of the following is a true statement about a pure parliamentary system of government?

(A) Legislators who accept ministerial appointments must resign their seats.
(B) Seats in parliament are apportioned strictly according to proportional representation.
(C) Governments must be formed by a coalition of several parties.
(D) The head of government must be a current member of the legislature.

GEOGRAPHY

Question 66 is based on the following map.

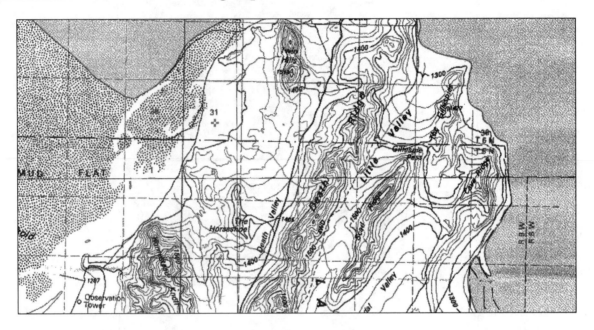

66. The map above is a

    (A) thematic map

    (B) topographic map

    (C) choropleth map

    (D) dot map

Question 67 is based on the following maps.

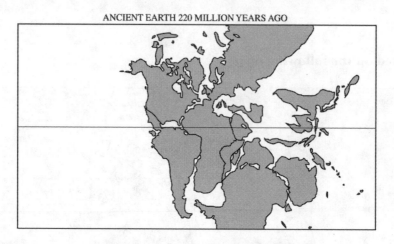

ANCIENT EARTH 220 MILLION YEARS AGO

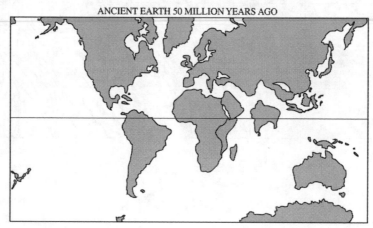

ANCIENT EARTH 50 MILLION YEARS AGO

67. According to the maps above, which of the following pair of modern-day regions is most likely to have similar geological attributes?

(A) South America and western Africa

(B) Western Australia and eastern South America

(C) Europe and Australia

(D) Eastern Asia and northern Africa

68. Which of the following rivers is NOT in Asia?

(A) Yangtze

(B) Mekong

(C) Euphrates

(D) Nile

Question 69 is based on the following map.

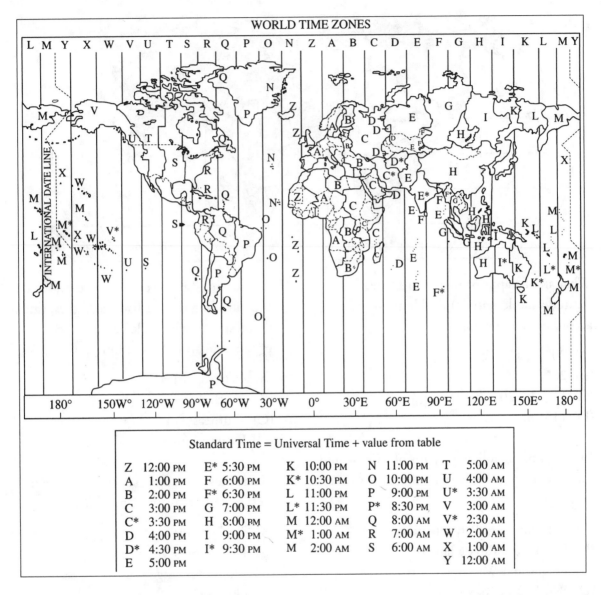

69. If it is 9:00 A.M. on Wednesday in Beijing, China, what day and time is it in Rio de Janeiro, Brazil?

(A) 10:00 A.M. Tuesday

(B) 10:00 P.M. Tuesday

(C) 10:00 A.M. Wednesday

(D) 10:00 P.M. Wednesday

Question 70 is based on the following map.

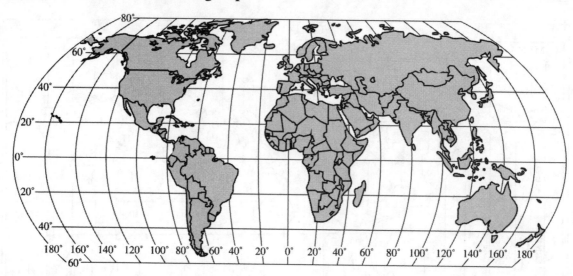

70. What are the approximate coordinates (latitude and longitude) for Hong Kong, according to the map?

    (A) 20° N, 115° E
    (B) 20° S, 115° W
    (C) 115° N, 20° W
    (D) 115° S, 20° E

71. In which of the following pairs of cities would inhabitants most likely share the same native language?

    (A) Barcelona and Port-au-Prince
    (B) Lisbon and Rio de Janeiro
    (C) Prague and Warsaw
    (D) Beijing and Tokyo

72. The Bosporus strait separates which of the following pairs of continents?

    (A) Europe and Africa
    (B) Africa and Asia
    (C) North America and South America
    (D) Europe and Asia

73. At the end of the twentieth century, which of the following regions had the highest rate of deforestation when calculated as a percentage of the total area of rain forest in the region?

    (A) Central Africa
    (B) South America
    (C) Southeast Asia
    (D) Eastern Europe

74. What causes weather patterns to move from west to east across the United States?

    (A) Trade winds
    (B) Jet stream
    (C) Mountain ranges
    (D) Gulf Stream

Question 75 is based on the following map.

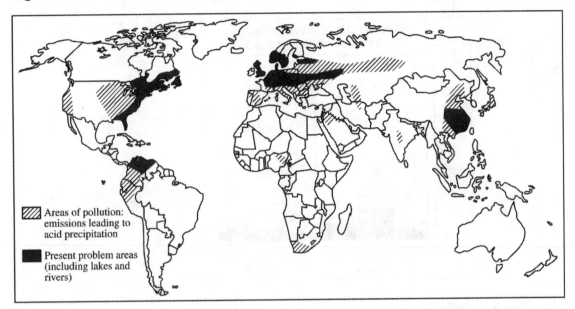

Areas of pollution:
emissions leading to
acid precipitation

Present problem areas
(including lakes and
rivers)

75. Which of the following most likely accounts
for the fact that acid precipitation may occur
far from its point of origin, as indicated by
the map?

(A) Prevailing winds
(B) Groundwater runoff
(C) Temperature fluctuation
(D) Depletion of the ozone layer

76. Which of the following regions is most closely
associated with the Islamic religion?

(A) South Asia
(B) Latin America
(C) Middle East
(D) Pacific Rim

Question 77 is based on the following graph.

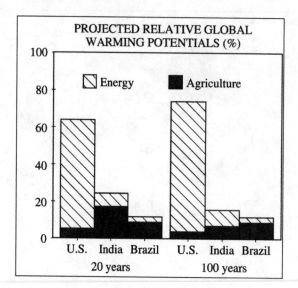

77. Which of the following conclusions is supported by the figures above?

   (A) The agricultural sectors of India and Brazil pose a greater long-term than short-term threat for increased global warming.

   (B) The energy sector of the United States poses a greater short- and long-term threat for increased global warming than the combined agricultural sectors of the United States, India, and Brazil.

   (C) While the short-term effects of Brazil's global warming potential may be significant, its long-term effects will be minimal.

   (D) The combined long-term global warming potential of India's agricultural sector poses a greater threat than the energy sector in the United States.

Question 78 is based on the following maps.

ARAL SEA IN 1960 AND 2000

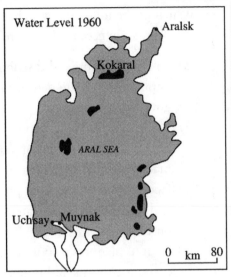 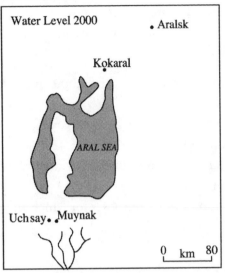

78. The massive depletion of the freshwater Aral Sea, which has shrunk from the fourth to the sixth largest lake in the world, is most likely due to which of the following?

   (A) Use of the water from the feeder rivers for irrigation
   (B) Occurrence of persistent drought in Kazakhstan
   (C) Effects of global warming
   (D) Increased dependence on groundwater mining

79. Which of the following countries, because its location made it unusually well placed to control trade during the Renaissance, rose to prominence in the 1700's?

   (A) Great Britain
   (B) France
   (C) Italy
   (D) Portugal

80. Which of the following has been a contributing factor in ethnic conflict and political unrest in sub-Saharan Africa during the last 50 years?

   (A) A higher-than-average rate of natural disasters
   (B) The Green Revolution
   (C) Colonial borders superimposed over a cultural mosaic
   (D) Rapid increase in literacy rates

ECONOMICS

81. Which of the following represents the opportunity cost of purchasing a used automobile for $6,000?

    (A) The difference between the $6,000 and the cost of a new car
    (B) The cost of paying for the necessary repairs to the car
    (C) The time it took to research and identify the appropriate used car
    (D) A vacation or other purposes for which the $6,000 could have been used

82. Assume that a country can produce both good X and good Y, but has a comparative advantage in the production of good X only. If the country specializes in the production of good X and imports good Y, the country will most likely consume

    (A) greater amounts of goods X and Y together than before trading
    (B) the same amounts of goods X and Y together as before trading
    (C) greater amounts of good X than before trading but smaller amounts of good Y
    (D) greater amounts of good Y than before trading but smaller amounts of good X

83. Which of the following is a characteristic of socialism as an economic system?

    (A) The production and distribution of the nation's output are determined by central government planners.
    (B) The decisions about production and distribution of the nation's output are made by individual households and firms.
    (C) Central planners impose production rules and regulations on privately owned businesses.
    (D) Central planners impose taxes on corporate profits and rents.

84. A firm that has market power to set the price for its product or service is

    (A) an individual proprietor
    (B) a corporation
    (C) a partnership
    (D) a monopoly

85. When compared with perfectly competitive firms in long-run equilibrium, a monopoly with an identical cost structure will charge a

    (A) higher price and produce lower output
    (B) higher price and produce higher output
    (C) lower price and produce higher output
    (D) lower price and produce lower output

Questions 86-87 are based on the following graph of supply and demand, which shows the market for a good.

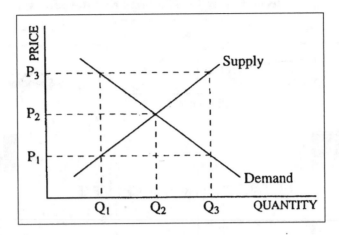

86. Assume a price ceiling was initially set at P_1. If the price ceiling is lifted (repealed), which of the following changes in the quantity demanded, quantity supplied, and price will occur?

	Quantity Demanded	Quantity Supplied	Price
(A)	Increase	Increase	Increase
(B)	Decrease	Increase	Increase
(C)	Increase	Decrease	Decrease
(D)	Decrease	Decrease	Decrease

87. Which of the following will occur if a price floor is set at P_3?

(A) There will be a shortage of (Q_2-Q_1) units of the good.

(B) There will be a shortage of (Q_3-Q_2) units of the good.

(C) There will be a surplus of (Q_3-Q_1) units of the good.

(D) There will be a surplus of (Q_2-Q_4) units of the good.

88. Which of the following is the best example of a perfectly competitive product market?

(A) A corn farmer who sells corn in the national commodity markets

(B) A single firm that sells a highly differentiated tennis shoe in the nation's retail stores

(C) A single company in competition with the United States Postal Service

(D) A company that hires its laborers from a single labor union pool

Question 89 is based on the following model.

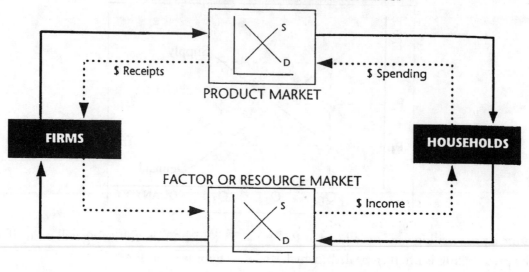

89. In the model, which of the following is a transaction that would occur in the factor or resource market?

(A) Consumers purchase products from local retailers.
(B) Firms hire employees to work in factories.
(C) Federal or state government agencies buy surplus agricultural products.
(D) Banks loan money to firms for investment.

90. In which of the following phases of the business cycle would the economy experience decreasing unemployment rates and increasing consumer spending?

    (A) Depression
    (B) Recession
    (C) Recovery
    (D) Contraction

91. Which of the following is an example of a progressive tax?

    (A) A tax that imposes a higher percentage rate of taxation on persons with lower incomes
    (B) A tax that imposes a higher percentage rate of taxation on persons with higher incomes
    (C) A tax that imposes the same percentage rate of taxation on everyone, regardless of income
    (D) A tax imposed on luxury goods rather than on necessities

92. Which of the following would most likely occur during periods of recession or depression?

    (A) Interest rates would increase by 5 to 10 percent.
    (B) Unemployment rates would increase by 5 to 10 percent.
    (C) Price levels would increase quarterly by about 3 percent.
    (D) Consumption of durable goods would increase quarterly by about 3 percent.

93. Assume that Country X is in a severe recession with an unemployment rate of 12 percent and declining growth. An economist would advocate which of the following fiscal policy actions to increase output and decrease unemployment?

	Action on Taxes	Action on Government Spending
(A)	Increase	Increase
(B)	Increase	Decrease
(C)	Decrease	Increase
(D)	Decrease	Decrease

94. In a period of inflation, which of the following combinations of monetary policy actions would the Federal Reserve most likely undertake?

	Discount Rate	Open-Market Operations
(A)	Decrease	Buy bonds
(B)	Decrease	Sell bonds
(C)	Increase	Buy bonds
(D)	Increase	Sell bonds

95. An increase in which of the following would be most likely to increase economic growth?

    (A) Productivity
    (B) Personal taxes
    (C) Consumer spending
    (D) Interest rates

96. Assume that the following represents the conditions of the economy for Country X.

	Year Ago	Month Ago	Today
Real gross domestic product (GDP)	1,800	1,770	1,770
Unemployment rate	3.5%	5.0%	7.0%
Private investment	301	285	285

According to the chart above, which of the following best characterizes the economic condition of Country X and an appropriate economic policy that could be recommended by fiscal policy makers?

	Condition of Country X	Economic Policy
(A)	Recession	Decrease personal taxes
(B)	Recession	Decrease government spending
(C)	Inflation	Increase personal taxes
(D)	Inflation	Increase government spending

Question 97 is based on the following chart.

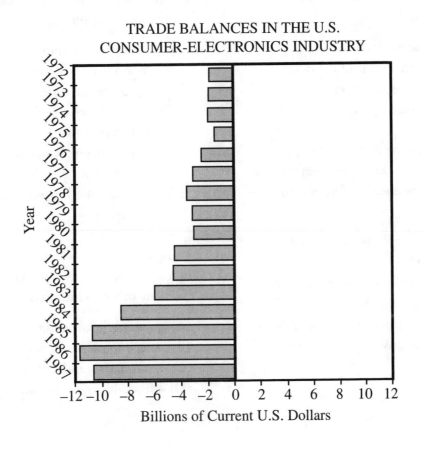

TRADE BALANCES IN THE U.S.
CONSUMER-ELECTRONICS INDUSTRY

97. Which of the following is consistent with the data shown in the chart above?

(A) The value of the United States dollar depreciated from 1972 to 1987.

(B) United States firms cut back on research and development of consumer electronics from 1972 to 1987.

(C) The United States imported more consumer electronics than it exported between 1972 and 1987.

(D) The Japanese have surpassed American output in consumer electronics.

98. Which of the following would necessarily increase if a nation imported more than it exported over time?

   (A) The current account deficit
   (B) The international value of the dollar
   (C) The growth of personal debt
   (D) The gross domestic product

99. Under a flexible exchange rate system, the international value of the United States dollar relative to other currencies is determined by the

   (A) amount of gold held by the United States Treasury
   (B) foreign demand for goods and services from the United States
   (C) current trade balance of the United States
   (D) current level of private debt in the United States

100. Which of the following is NOT likely to be given as a justification for establishing protective tariffs on imports?

   (A) To allow infant industries time to develop within their own countries
   (B) To provide the widest possible variety of goods and services within the country
   (C) To guarantee that sufficient supplies of essential materials will be available in times of crisis
   (D) To preserve high-paying jobs within the home country

101. Using a unit of the same resource, a nation that can produce more of a given product than any other country has

   (A) an absolute advantage
   (B) an economic dependence
   (C) a comparative advantage
   (D) a favorable trade balance

Question 102 is based on the following chart, which shows the exchange rate value of the British pound and Japanese yen per United States dollar on two different dates.

Exchange Rate of a United States Dollar

	February 1	March 1
British pound	£0.586	£0.569
Japanese yen	¥118.2	¥119.1

102. According to the data above, what happened to the value of the United States dollar relative to the British pound and the Japanese yen between February 1 and March 1 ?

(A) The dollar appreciated with respect to the British pound and the Japanese yen.

(B) The dollar appreciated with respect to the British pound but depreciated with respect to the Japanese yen.

(C) The dollar depreciated with respect to the British pound but appreciated with respect to the Japanese yen.

(D) The dollar depreciated with respect to the British pound and the Japanese yen.

103. What was the major purpose of the North American Free Trade Agreement (NAFTA)?

(A) To protect labor unions in the United States, Canada, and Mexico

(B) To increase energy production in the United States, Canada, and Mexico

(C) To reduce tariffs and other trade barriers among the United States, Canada, and Mexico

(D) To increase trade between North America and the European Union

BEHAVIORAL SCIENCES

Note: The behavioral sciences are **not** covered in the *Citizenship Education* test. If you are going to take the *Citizenship Education* test, you do not need to take questions 104-117.

104. According to B. F. Skinner's theories, which of the following should be used to increase the frequency of a behavior?

    (A) Latent learning
    (B) Positive reinforcement
    (C) Punishment
    (D) Classical conditioning

105. "Normally, there is nothing of which we are more certain than the feeling of our self, of our own ego. This ego appears to us as something autonomous and unitary, marked off distinctly from everything else. That such an appearance is deceptive, and that on the contrary the ego is continued inwards, without any sharp delimitation, into an unconscious mental entity which we designate as the id and for which it serves as a kind of façade—this was a discovery first made by psychoanalytic research, which should still have much more to tell us about the relation of the ego to the id."

    The ideas expressed in this excerpt are most closely associated with which of the following thinkers?

    (A) Abraham Maslow
    (B) Jean Piaget
    (C) Ivan Pavlov
    (D) Sigmund Freud

106. Which of the following has grown in importance in the United States as an agent of socialization during the twentieth century?

    (A) The media
    (B) Religion
    (C) Government
    (D) Voluntary associations

107. Vertical social mobility would be most fluid in a society whose social stratification is based primarily on

    (A) lineage
    (B) income
    (C) gender
    (D) race

108. Which of the following is a major social institution?

    (A) Religion
    (B) Community
    (C) Entertainment
    (D) Technology

Question 109 is based on the following photograph.

From *City of Quartz: Excavating the Future in Los Angeles,*
by Mike Davis, photographs by Robert Morrow.
Copyright © by Verso, an imprint of
New Left Books, London.

109. The photograph above reflects which of the following demographic trends in Los Angeles in the 1990's?

(A) An increasing proportion of young adults between the ages of 18 and 24

(B) Decreasing numbers of self-employed entrepreneurs

(C) A decreasing rate of literacy

(D) Increasing ethnic diversity

110. The relationship between prejudice and discrimination is best characterized by which of the following?

    (A) Stereotype and generalization
    (B) Faith and values
    (C) Morality and law
    (D) Attitude and action

111. Which of the following is an example of discrimination?

    (A) Disliking a next-door neighbor because of race
    (B) Refusing to allow a gay couple to adopt a child
    (C) Being suspicious of a person because of ethnicity
    (D) Feeling uncomfortable around an interracial couple

Question 112 is based on the following photograph.

AP
Wide World Photos

112. The photo above of the 1963 March on Washington represents which of the following solutions to a contemporary social problem?

(A) Military mobilization
(B) Nonviolent protest
(C) Sit-down strike
(D) Patriotic rally

113. According to psychologists, the most important developmental task during adolescence is

(A) motor-skill formation
(B) suppressing emotions
(C) identity formation
(D) maintaining secure attachments

114. Which of the following is the most common psychological disorder in the United States?

(A) Major depressive disorder
(B) Schizophrenia
(C) Paranoid personality disorder
(D) Dissociative identity disorder

Question 115 is based on the following graph.

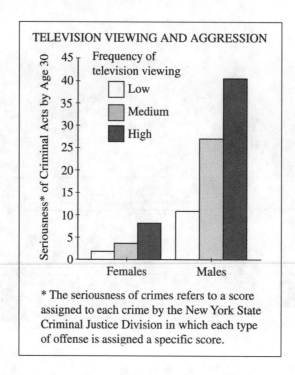

TELEVISION VIEWING AND AGGRESSION

* The seriousness of crimes refers to a score assigned to each crime by the New York State Criminal Justice Division in which each type of offense is assigned a specific score.

115. Which of the following conclusions is supported by the chart above?

(A) There is no definite correlation between frequency of television viewing and the commission of serious crimes.

(B) Frequent television viewing causes the commission of serious crimes.

(C) The commission of serious crimes increases the frequency of television viewing.

(D) The commission of serious crimes positively correlates with the frequency of television viewing.

116. Communities of Hasidic Jews living in New York City and Mennonites living in rural Ohio are both examples of

(A) utopias
(B) subcultures
(C) reactionary groups
(D) dominant societies

117. When trade and ancient warfare brought ancient Egypt into contact with others, many of these civilizations adopted Egyptian ideas, cultures, and technologies. The term that describes this process is known as

(A) cultural diffusion
(B) socialization
(C) social stratification
(D) culture clash

Chapter 12

Right Answers and Explanations
for the Practice Questions

▶   ▶   ▶   ▶   ▶   ▶   ▶   ▶   ▶   ▶   ▶   ▶

Right Answers and Explanations for the Practice Questions

Now that you have answered all of the practice questions, you can check your work.
Compare your answers with the correct answers in the table below.

Question Number	Correct Answer	Content Category	Question Number	Correct Answer	Content Category
1	D	Physical Geography of North America	49	C	Basic Political Concepts
2	B	Physical Geography of North America	50	D	Basic Political Concepts
3	A	Physical Geography of North America	51	B	Basic Political Concepts
4	C	Native American Peoples	52	A	Basic Political Concepts
5	B	Native American Peoples	53	B	United States Political System
6	D	European Exploration and Colonization	54	D	United States Political System
7	A	European Exploration and Colonization	55	C	United States Political System
8	C	Establishing a New Nation	56	A	United States Political System
9	B	Establishing a New Nation	57	A	United States Political System
10	A	Establishing a New Nation	58	D	United States Political System
11	D	Establishing a New Nation	59	B	United States Political System
12	C	Continued National Development	60	D	United States Political System
13	A	Continued National Development	61	C	United States Political System
14	C	Civil War Era	62	D	Systems of Government/International Politics
15	B	Civil War Era	63	A	Systems of Government/International Politics
16	A	Emergence of the Modern United States	64	D	Systems of Government/International Politics
17	C	Emergence of the Modern United States	65	D	Systems of Government/International Politics
18	B	Progressive Era through the New Deal	66	B	The World in Spatial Terms
19	B	The Second World War and the Postwar Period	67	A	The World in Spatial Terms
20	C	The Second World War and the Postwar Period	68	D	The World in Spatial Terms
21	A	The Second World War and the Postwar Period	69	B	The World in Spatial Terms
22	D	Recent Developments	70	A	Places and Regions
23	C	Recent Developments	71	B	Places and Regions
24	A	Human Society to ca. 3500 B.C.E.	72	D	Places and Regions
25	D	Human Society to ca. 3500 B.C.E.	73	C	Physical Systems
26	C	Development of City Civilizations	74	B	Physical Systems
27	A	Development of City Civilizations	75	A	Physical Systems
28	B	Ancient Empires and Civilizations	76	C	Human Systems
29	C	Ancient Empires and Civilizations	77	B	Environment and Society
30	A	Ancient Empires and Civilizations	78	A	Environment and Society
31	C	Ancient Empires and Civilizations	79	A	The Uses of Geography
32	B	Disruption and Reversal	80	C	The Uses of Geography
33	A	Disruption and Reversal	81	D	Fundamental Concepts
34	B	Disruption and Reversal	82	A	Fundamental Concepts
35	C	Emerging Global Interaction	83	A	Fundamental Concepts
36	B	Emerging Global Interaction	84	D	Fundamental Concepts
37	D	Emerging Global Interaction	85	A	Microeconomics
38	B	Emerging Global Interaction	86	B	Microeconomics
39	A	Emerging Global Interaction	87	C	Microeconomics
40	B	Political and Industrial Revolutions, Nationalism	88	A	Microeconomics
41	C	Political and Industrial Revolutions, Nationalism	89	B	Microeconomics
42	D	Political and Industrial Revolutions, Nationalism	90	C	Macroeconomics
43	C	Conflicts, Ideologies, and Revolutions in the Twentieth Century	91	B	Macroeconomics
44	D	Conflicts, Ideologies, and Revolutions in the Twentieth Century	92	B	Macroeconomics
45	A	Conflicts, Ideologies, and Revolutions in the Twentieth Century	93	C	Macroeconomics
46	D	Contemporary Trends	94	D	Macroeconomics
47	B	Basic Political Concepts	95	A	Macroeconomics
48	D	Basic Political Concepts	96	A	Macroeconomics

Question Number	Correct Answer	Content Category	Question Number	Correct Answer	Content Category
97	C	International Economic Concepts	108	A	Sociology
98	A	International Economic Concepts	109	D	Sociology
99	B	International Economic Concepts	110	D	Sociology
100	B	International Economic Concepts	111	B	Sociology
101	A	International Economic Concepts	112	B	Sociology
102	C	International Economic Concepts	113	C	Psychology
103	C	Current Issues and Controversies	114	A	Psychology
104	B	Psychology	115	D	Psychology
105	D	Psychology	116	B	Anthropology
106	A	Sociology	117	A	Anthropology
107	B	Sociology			

Explanations of Right Answers

UNITED STATES HISTORY

1. This question tests your ability to recognize the characteristics of various geographic regions of the United States. The southwestern United States is characterized by dry climate; most areas there receive less than 16 inches of rain per year. As a result, agriculture is possible in most parts of the Southwest only with irrigation, in contrast to the other regions mentioned. The correct answer, therefore, is (D).

2. This question tests your knowledge of important geographic locations in the United States. Of the states listed as possible answers, Michigan is adjacent to four of the Great Lakes, New York borders two, and Pennsylvania one. The correct answer, therefore, is (B).

3. This question tests your ability to recognize the characteristics of various geographic regions of the United States. The southeastern United States has a humid subtropical climate, typified by abundant rainfall, hot summers, and mild winters. Both the Mediterranean and tropical savanna climates have significant dry seasons during the year, while the desert climate is characterized by very limited annual rainfall. The correct answer, therefore, is (A).

4. This questions tests your knowledge of Native American–colonial relations in the pre-Revolutionary era. The encroachment of European settlers into lands controlled by tribes of the Iroquois Six Nations caused growing resentment among Native Americans during the early 1750's. The correct answer, therefore, is (C).

5. This question tests your knowledge of major events during the period of continued national development in the United States. Asserting that the federal government could not mediate sovereignty disputes between states and Indian nations, President Andrew Jackson prevailed upon Congress to pass a law providing for the removal of Native Americans living east of the Appalachian Mountains to federal lands west of the Mississippi River. The Cherokee Indians appealed to the Supreme Court and won, yet they were still marched by the United States Army from Georgia to Oklahoma along the infamous "Trail of Tears." The correct answer, therefore, is (B).

6. This question tests your ability to identify an important factual connection between two events during the period of European exploration and colonization. European explorers introduced a host of epidemic diseases to the native populations they encountered upon their arrival in North America. With no immunity from these foreign illnesses, indigenous peoples died in tremendous numbers from smallpox, measles, and other contagious diseases. The correct answer, therefore, is (D).

7. This question tests your ability to recognize important ideas and events in pre-Revolutionary America. This quotation, taken from a famous sermon by the Connecticut minister Jonathan Edwards, exemplifies the emphasis on sin and the need for personal conversion that lay at the heart of the First Great Awakening, a far-reaching Protestant religious revival that lasted from the mid-1730's to the early 1740's. The correct answer, therefore, is (A).

8. This question tests your knowledge of political ideas and events in the early years of the new nation. The men who met in Philadelphia in 1787 to draft the Constitution drew on the ideals of the ancient Roman republic to establish a new government for the United States, which included indirect representation through a bicameral legislature and an independent executive. The correct answer, therefore, is (C).

9. This question tests your ability to recognize key elements of governmental policy during the Revolutionary period in American history. The Articles of Confederation represented the first attempt to provide for an American national government but were beset by shortcomings, many of them stemming from the reluctance of delegates to the Continental Congress to relinquish state power in favor of a strong federal authority. The resulting government was hampered by numerous restrictions, among the most serious of which was the inability to levy taxes. The correct answer, therefore, is (B).

10. This question tests your ability to interpret a political statement from the period of continued national development in the United States. In this passage, the author argues that tolerating the oppression and violence inherent in the slave system can make citizens less willing to support republican principles of equality. The correct answer, therefore, is (A).

11. This question tests your knowledge of the political ideologies of some of the major figures in the early years of the new nation as well as your ability to interpret a short historical text. Thomas Jefferson strongly believed that the United States should adhere to its agrarian past, with the "yeoman farmer" (a farmer who works his own small farm) serving as his model for the ideal citizen. This view contrasted sharply with the perspectives of the three other men listed above, especially Hamilton, who favored industrial development and extensive foreign trade as the basis for America's economy. The correct answer, therefore, is (D).

12. This question tests your ability to identify and distinguish among important mid-nineteenth-century social reform movements. Although increased political activism by women during the 1840's led to the first Women's Rights Convention, held in 1848 in Seneca Falls, New York, the movement had difficulty gaining members and was unable to influence public attitudes to the same extent as the temperance, public education, and abolition movements. The correct answer, therefore, is (C).

13. This question tests your ability to interpret a visual aid while drawing on your knowledge of United States politics in the decades leading up to the Civil War. The mid-nineteenth-century expansionist movement in America held that it was the "Manifest destiny" of the United States to spread across the continent, so that White settlers could take over the "empty" lands of the West, like those shown in the background of the picture. The correct answer, therefore, is (A).

14. This question tests your ability to recognize the major characteristics of proslavery ideology in a historical text from the antebellum period of American history. In a famous speech delivered on the floor of the Senate in March

1858, James H. Hammond of South Carolina, arguing in defense of slavery, asserted to his colleagues that the United States—like all civilized societies—needed a so-called "mudsill" to provide basic labor for America's upper class. The correct answer, therefore, is (C).

15. This question tests your ability to recognize an important connection between a publication and a movement during the Civil War era. Published in 1852 by Harriet Beecher Stowe, the daughter of a prominent theologian, *Uncle Tom's Cabin* invigorated the abolitionist movement in the northern United States with its sharply critical portrayal of slavery. The correct answer, therefore, is (B).

16. This question tests your ability to analyze a cartoon and recognize its relationship to politics in the late nineteenth century. This 1872 drawing by the famous political cartoonist Thomas Nast criticizes the corruption of elected officials and civil servants in the post–Civil War period. The Pendleton Act, passed by Congress in 1883, took aim at political fraud and bribery by mandating competitive examinations for bureaucratic positions. The correct answer, therefore, is (A).

17. This question tests your ability to analyze a quotation and understand its significance to a political or social movement. Alarmed by the debilitating working conditions in United States factories at the end of the nineteenth century, activists belonging to organizations such as the American Federation of Labor urged the government to introduce a variety of workplace reforms. One of the most important, and contested, of these was the

eight-hour workday, which was passed by Congress in 1916. Lower tariffs and the gold standard were generally supported by factory owners, not labor activists. Relocation of factories overseas was not occurring in the early twentieth century, and would have been opposed by labor activists anyway. The correct answer, therefore, is (C).

18. This question tests your ability to understand a song lyric and recognize its relationship to an event in American history. The description of "khaki suits" in the first line of the stanza alludes to the military uniform of the First World War while the line "Brother can you spare a dime" refers to the economic hardship many veterans faced during the Great Depression. Together they suggest the correct answer, which is (B).

19. This question tests your ability to identify the key element of a mid-twentieth-century court decision. In 1954 the Supreme Court ruled that the practice of school segregation, defended by some as creating separate but equal educational environments, was in fact a violation of the United States Constitution. This decision came to serve as the legal basis for a host of challenges to discriminatory practices in American social and political institutions. The correct answer, therefore, is (B).

20. This question asks you to analyze a quotation and assess its relationship to a mid-twentieth-century political movement. Joseph McCarthy, a Republican senator from Wisconsin, was the among the most ardent anti-Communist politicians of his generation, famous for his 1950 assertion that the State Department was

dominated by Communists, an accusation that led to congressional hearings on the matter. The correct answer, therefore, is (C).

21. This question tests your knowledge of United States–Soviet relations during the Cold War. In October 1962 President John F. Kennedy ordered a naval blockade to prevent the Soviet Union from installing nuclear missiles on the island of Cuba. Unlike the other examples listed above, the Cuban missile crisis brought the two nations into direct conflict with one another, a departure from the usual Cold War pattern of confrontation through surrogate nations, such as Vietnam and Korea. Also, unlike the Korean and Vietnam Wars, the resolution of the Cuban missile crisis was widely seen as a clear United States success. The correct answer, therefore, is (A).

22. This question asks you to correctly interpret historical changes shown by means of graphs and to identify a factor contributing to those changes. The graphs show two interrelated trends, a decline in the number of farms between 1940 and 1990 and an increase in the average size of farms in the same period. Many factors contributed to these trends, but a major one was the increased use of agricultural machinery, which made it more efficient to farm large tracts of land. Despite federal subsidies to small farmers, family farms were increasingly replaced by large agribusinesses, which could produce crops more cheaply. Agricultural prices varied greatly in between 1940 and 1990, but were generally driven downward, not upward, by mechanization. The correct answer, therefore, is (D).

23. This question tests your knowledge of important events and figures in the Civil Rights movement of the 1950's and 1960's in the United States. On December 1, 1955, an African American woman named Rosa Parks refused to give up her seat to a White man on a bus in Montgomery, Alabama. Her arrest prompted African Americans to organize a boycott of the city's buses, which contributed to the emergence of the Reverend Martin Luther King Jr. as a prominent leader in the Civil Rights cause. The correct answer, therefore, is (C).

WORLD HISTORY

24. This question asks you about human origins. Scholars disagree about whether we *(Homo sapiens)* originated in one place and spread throughout the world or whether *Homo sapiens* developed from *Homo erectus* in several different world regions independently. New genetic evidence seems to support the former theory, but this evidence is still highly controversial. There is, however, general agreement that *Homo sapiens'* immediate ancestor, *Homo erectus,* appeared first in Africa about one million years ago and spread from there to Asia and, perhaps, to Europe. The correct answer, therefore, is (A).

25. This question asks you to examine a work of art and relate that work to the type of society that produced it. The work is an example of the many thousands of cave paintings produced in the Paleolithic period or Old Stone Age. Very little is known about the purpose of the paintings. Most early historians speculate that the cave paintings were part of

rituals to ensure the success of a hunt. It is known that the peoples of the Paleolithic period were organized as hunting and gathering societies. Peoples of this era depended on large- and small-scale animal hunts and on foraging natural plants. Agriculture and herding came later in time. The correct answer, therefore, is (D).

26. This question asks you to identify an ancient civilization by assessing a description of its major characteristics. Only Ancient Egypt possessed all of the characteristics described: an organized system of government, a polytheistic religion, a sophisticated method of irrigation, and a unique pictorial writing known as hieroglyphics. The correct answer, therefore, is (C).

27. This question asks you to interpret a map of early civilizations. The map shows that most of the early civilizations centered in river valleys and along coasts. Although (B), (C), and (D) might be true statements about some early civilizations, they are not true of most nor are they supported directly by the map provided. The correct answer, therefore, is (A).

28. This question asks you to identify a major world religion by giving you four of its basic tenets. The four "truths" outlined in the question, known as the Four Noble Truths, are the basis of Buddhism. Prince Siddhartha Gautama (around 563 to around 480 B.C.E.) of India is said to have engaged in intense meditation and perceived the connections between past lives and the present and the way to enlightenment, thus becoming the Buddha, or the "one who is enlightened." (A), (C), and (D) do not focus on suffering,

desire, and enlightenment. The correct answer, therefore, is (B).

29. This question tests your ability to recognize a major characteristic of Indian mathematics. The Indian system of place-value notation was much more efficient than the unwieldy numerical systems of the Egyptians, Greeks, and Romans, and the concept of zero (also developed by Mayan society) is widely considered to be a profound intellectual achievement that must be ranked as one of the most important and influential discoveries in human history. The Indian method of arithmetic had separate columns for ones, tens, hundreds, and so forth, as well as a zero sign to indicate the absence of units in a given column. This system made it possible to express very large numbers economically. This Indian system spread to the Middle East, Southeast Asia, and East Asia by the seventh century. Europe did not receive the technology until around the tenth century, when several European scholars became exposed to the mathematics of the Arabs. The correct answer, therefore, is (C).

30. This question asks you to make a comparison between Athens and Sparta at the beginning of the Peloponnesian War. Choices (B), (C), and (D) apply to both Sparta and Athens, but choice (A) points to a sharp distinction between the two city-states. Spartans lived a regimented life in which individualism was punished with exile or death to preserve the common good. Accumulation of wealth and expansion of trade were looked down on, and traditional aristocratic values were honored. Athens, in contrast, celebrated and protected individual freedoms for male citizens and valued trade and international exchange. The correct answer, therefore, is (A).

31. This question asks you to identify the major characteristics of the Augustan Roman Empire. Notice that this is an EXCEPT question, asking you to choose the single characteristic among the choices that did *not* characterize the Roman Empire after it was reorganized by Augustus. Augustus, known for his keen administrative talent, transformed the political structure of ancient Rome essentially into an imperial dynasty. Augustus effectively consolidated the legislative, military, financial, and religious powers of Rome into one-man rule, under the title of emperor. Because of the efficiency of the 44-year rule of Augustus and the reluctance of both the citizens and the Roman Senate to return to the pre-Augustan political chaos of highly competitive military rivals, the emperorship became a traditional hereditary position within the Roman state. The Roman state after Augustus' reorganization was marked by increased trade and the spread of Roman law, as well as overcrowding and pollution that affected Rome's lower classes. The Roman state and economy, however, consistently relied on slave labor, although slaves could conduct business and some were able to buy their freedom. The correct answer, therefore, is (C).

32. This question asks you to identify an important result of the European participation in the Crusades. The Crusaders were a burden to the Byzantines and at one point pillaged the Byzantine capital of Constantinople. Pope Urban II intended to strengthen his moral, military, and economic position by means of a Crusade, but the results were just the opposite. Eurasian trade routes remained under the control of the Byzantine Empire, Arab states, and a variety of other powers. The European Crusades to the Middle East had significant economic and cultural impacts. Pilgrims returning home introduced new foods, ideas, and technology, all of which helped to stimulate exchange between the eastern and the western Mediterranean. The correct answer, therefore, is (B).

33. This question asks you to look at a map of Africa in the period 1200 through 1600 and explain what the map shows. Using the map and additional knowledge, you would identify a significant connection between the trade routes shown and the major cultural development of the period—the spread of Islam in Africa, primarily by trade. Most of these routes are generally considered a crucial means for the spread of beliefs and technologies (as well as goods) between Asia and Africa. Europe had very little contact with any part of Africa except North Africa during this period. The major empires and civilizations of Africa did not unite during this period. The correct answer, therefore, is (A).

34. This question asks you to recall a major socioeconomic pattern that characterized both Europe and Japan. Feudal societies were characterized by a decentralized administration that indicated a weakened monarchical or imperial control, with regional leaders (members of an aristocratic warrior-elite) who gave something of value—land or money—to knights or samurai in exchange for loyalty and military support. Both Europe and Japan had such systems, including codes of knightly or samurai behavior. The correct answer, therefore, is (B).

35. This question asks you how a work of art can help interpret the context of the European Renaissance. The European Renaissance was characterized by the development of humanism, a system of thought based on the study of human ideas and actions. Humanists explored human endeavors in their art, literature, and poetry. Artists and thinkers of the Renaissance rediscovered the Classical world's emphasis on the individual in art and philosophy. Although many Renaissance artists explored religious subjects in their work, they often created works through the lens of humanistic values, with much attention given to human form and individual expression. The correct answer, therefore, is (C).

36. This question asks you to examine a work of art and generalize from the work. In this instance, you are asked to generalize about the artist's attitude toward nature and how it typifies the society's attitude toward nature. The view of nature in Japan is quite different from that of Western societies. Choice (A) illustrates the Western view during the scientific revolution and the Enlightenment. Choices (C) and (D) are typical of certain philosophies, but not of those of East Asia. In Asian societies nature is seen as powerful whereas humankind is not. Control of nature to any great degree is not possible. In addition, humans can draw strength from nature. The correct answer, therefore, is (B).

37. This question asks you to recognize major reactions of the Catholic Church to the Protestant Reformation. Notice that this is an EXCEPT question, asking you to choose the single reaction among the choices that was *not* one of the Church's reactions. The Church reacted to the Protestant call for reform both

defensively, by prohibiting Protestant reform books and by renouncing reformers as heretics, and positively, by supporting the arts to glorify the Catholic religion. In addition, the Church instituted reforms and reaffirmed major doctrines (Council of Trent). The translation of the Bible into vernacular languages, however, was primarily a Protestant endeavor not supported by the Catholic Church at that time. The correct answer, therefore, is (D).

38. This question asks you to understand a quotation about the French Revolution (1789–1804), a movement characterized by both massive violence and significant social and political change. Tocqueville writes that the nobility allowed taxation without consent as long as the nobility itself remained free from taxation. Tocqueville indicates that this unjust "bargain" was the start of all the vices and abuses by the monarchy and the nobility that ultimately culminated in the French Revolution. The correct answer, therefore, is (B).

39. This question asks you to read a quotation and identify its historical context. Hernán Cortés left Cuba in 1519 with 600 soldiers and a stock of weaponry and horses in order to assault the Aztec Empire in central Mexico. Both the horses that the soldiers rode on and the visitors themselves were initially strange to the Mexican peoples, who had had no previous contact with Europeans. The correct answer, therefore, is (A).

40. This question asks you to identify the major political ideas expressed in a particular document. Karl Marx's and Friedrich Engels' *Communist Manifesto* expresses the basis of socialism. Marx believed that the capitalistic system allowed the bourgeoisie (the owners of

businesses and factories) to exploit the proletariat (the working class). Ultimately, Marx and Engels believed this tension between the bourgeoisie and the proletariat would lead to revolution. The correct answer, therefore, is (B).

41. This question asks you to interpret a cartoon and a quotation in their historical context. The cartoon underscores the physically demanding and dirty work performed by women in the mines of the nineteenth century, while the quotation, on the other hand, reflects the gender ideals that were emerging in Victorian England. Victorian morality claimed to be universal, but it best fit European upper- and middle-class families. Although the lives of middle-class Victorian women were a mixture of luxury and discrimination, working-class women, by contrast, led lives of physical toil and pain. The correct answer, therefore, is (C).

42. This question tests your ability to interpret a political cartoon in its historical context. The cartoon depicts leaders of several European countries forming "matches" for a game of badminton. The "game of the day" that the title refers to is the game of political alliance-making, a game in which Germany, France, Italy, Russia, Great Britain, Japan, the Ottoman Empire, and Austria-Hungary participated in the decades preceding the First World War. The alliance blocs created by these countries entangled the world and ultimately contributed to the global nature of the First World War. The correct answer, therefore, is (D).

43. This question asks you to recognize the characteristics of an important historical event. Strongly influenced by Western ideas and practices, Mao Zedong helped found the communist movement in China. The Communists had established a base area in the Kiangsi Province in southeast China. Mao had a leading role at the Jiangxi base but had been removed from a leadership role by the Communist Party Central Committee before the Nationalist Army attacks, forcing the communists to begin the famous Long March (1934–1935) described in the quotation cited in the question. The March solidified Mao's return to the leadership of the party. The correct answer, therefore, is (C).

44. This question asks you to analyze a political cartoon in its historical context. The cartoon shows a Nazi tank coming face-to-face with a ghostly image of Napoleon mounted on a horse. Both Hitler and Napoleon were ultimately stopped by the sheer brutality of the Russian winter, a brutality which neither had sufficiently accounted for, and the size and persistence of the Russian army. The correct answer, therefore, is (D).

45. This question asks you to recognize one aspect of the philosophy of a major historical figure. While attending the Crozer Theological Seminary in Pennsylvania, Martin Luther King Jr. became familiar with Mohandas Gandhi, who had struggled to free the people of India from British rule by "peaceful revolution." King led the civil rights movement in the United States until his assassination in 1968. The correct answer, therefore, is (A).

46. This question asks you to look at contemporary global politics and explain a general trend. During the period, conflicts did not lessen despite indications that global interdependence on the political and economic

level is key to every nation's health. The disintegration of the Soviet Union led to Russia's inability to play a leading role in international peacekeeping, and Russia's relations with the United States did not become close enough for ongoing joint military actions. The United Nations, the United States, and NATO acted in many areas to prevent the spread of conflict and to reach lasting settlements of differences, though not necessarily with success—some examples are Yugoslavia, Somalia, and Haiti. The correct answer, therefore, is (D).

GOVERNMENT AND CIVICS

47. This question tests your basic knowledge of political ideologies. In political terminology, liberalism centers on individual liberties and rights and their protection by the state. While conservatives can champion individual rights and liberties, they do not center on the role of the state in the protection of those freedoms. The correct answer, therefore, is (B).

48. This question asks you to understand an excerpt from a text of political philosophy and recognize its relationship to a major political theory. Karl Marx, the famous German philosopher, social revolutionary, and political economist, published his *Communist Manifesto* in 1848. All of history, he argued, is the struggle between those who control the means of production and those who work for them, classes that he referred to as the bourgeoisie and the proletariat. He called for the overthrow of the established order to remedy this situation, and the formation of a Communist Party to stimulate proletarian

class-consciousness. The correct answer, therefore, is (D).

49. This question asks you to recognize the connection between the idea of the "consent of the governed" and an important philosopher, John Locke. His most significant work on political philosophy, *Two Treatises of Government,* is a refutation of the divine rights of kings and the absolutist theory of government. Locke saw government as existing only for the public good, and the ruler's authority as conditional rather than absolute. The correct answer, therefore, is (C).

50. This question asks you to recognize a violation of the constitutional arrangement of government. The refusal of a subnational government (such as a state government) to obey national law implies that the state does not consider the national law to be legitimate and, by implication, that the subnational government does not consider the national government to be legitimate. The correct answer, therefore, is (D).

51. This question tests your knowledge of major political theories. In 1651 Thomas Hobbes published *Leviathan,* in which he articulated the beginnings of social contract theory. In that work he presented a view of humanity as existing by nature in a "war of all against all," from which we emerge by giving up the freedoms we are born with in exchange for protection by a sovereign. Locke's work later in the century articulated a different view of social contract, arguing that the only legitimate government is one to which people consent in order to protect their rights under natural law. The correct answer, therefore, is (B).

52. This question tests your knowledge of an important political term. Federalism is characterized by the sharing of power between a central national government and state or local governments. (B) is incorrect because under federalism, subgovernments have some degree of independent authority and responsibilities that are not merely delegated by the national government. Choice (C) describes a confederal arrangement of sovereign countries, such as the European Union. Choice (D) is not relevant to the definition of federalism. The correct answer, therefore, is (A).

53. This question asks you to recognize the important political term "interest groups" and to understand the function of these groups. Interest groups are aggregates of individuals based on a limited range of shared concerns. They promote their policy agenda, in large part by providing legislators and policy makers with specialized information on issues that involve the interest groups' goals. The correct answer, therefore, is (B).

54. This question asks you to recognize an important aspect of American party politics by analyzing the opinion presented in the quotation. One of the most important effects of significant third-party candidacies is that they can force one or both of the two dominant parties to shift their political platforms. A third-party candidate who appeals to the hard right, for example, may threaten to pull votes from the Republican candidate. The Republican candidate is likely to respond by adding more conservative planks to the platform in order to retain those votes. The correct answer, therefore, is (D).

55. This question tests your understanding of the structure of government as determined by the United States Constitution. The Constitution organizes the basic powers of the three branches of government. The President's formal responsibilities include acting as chief executive and commander in chief of the armed forces, as well as the ability to make treaties. The actual ratification of treaties and declarations of war are left to Congress, which has the responsibility to make laws. The judicial branch has the responsibility of ruling on the constitutionality of laws. Among the limited powers of the President granted by the Constitution is the ability to grant pardons for offenses against the country. The correct answer, therefore, is (C).

56. This question tests your recognition of the purpose of the Bill of Rights. The first ten amendments to the United States Constitution, the Bill of Rights, derive from the colonial struggle against the King of England and Parliament, as well as growing concepts of individual equality. They constitute a collection of mutually reinforcing guarantees of individual rights and limitations on national government power. The correct answer, therefore, is (A).

57. This question asks you to recognize an important social and demographic characteristic of the United States political electorate. While average voter turnout has recently ranged from 36 to 55 percent of the voting-age population, the 18-to-24-year-old age bracket had voter turnout of 32 percent or less. It has consistently been the case in recent years that the 18-to-24-year-old age-group has the lowest election turnout of all age-groups in the United States. The correct answer, therefore, is (A).

58. This question asks you to recognize a major issue in electoral politics in the United States. Voter turnout is the rate at which eligible voters actually appear at the polls to cast their ballot during elections. Turnout in the United States has been significantly lower than in most other developed democracies. The correct answer, therefore, is (D).

59. This question tests your knowledge of important rules in the legislative branch of the United States government. The allowance of unlimited debate in the Senate reflects a key distinction between the chambers of Congress. The ability to filibuster, or to hold up action on a bill by refusing to yield the floor, gives individual senators a degree of influence over legislation that is not available to members of the House, whose debate is governed by a more restrictive set of rules. The correct answer, therefore, is (B).

60. This question tests your knowledge of one aspect of checks and balances in the United States government. While Congress gives federal agencies authority over numerous programs, Congress continues to verify that the bureaucracy is carrying out the intent of federal programs. This is known as legislative oversight. There is a number of congressional tools for oversight, including the budgeting process and committee hearings. The correct answer is (D), which is an example of a committee hearing about a federal agency.

61. This question tests your knowledge of how the federal government allocates funds to states. Federal funding is often given to the states in the forms of both categorical grants and block grants. Categorical grants earmark the funds for specific uses and often require that the

states meet a number of other requirements to receive and use these funds. Block grants give the states more discretion in that they provide federal funds for general areas of use but allow the states to implement the specifics of the programs. The correct answer, therefore, is (C).

62. This question asks you to recognize the relationship between the concepts found in the quotation and the political policy of isolationism. Isolationism is a policy of national isolation from world affairs by generally abstaining from alliances and other types of international political relations. The author of the quote argues that the United States should abstain from interfering with ethnic conflicts overseas, leaving the task to the United Nations. This most closely resembles isolationism, making (D) the correct answer.

63. This question asks you to recognize the definition of an important political term, direct democracy. In a representative democracy, as in the United States, voters elect representatives who in turn make political decisions. In a direct democracy, the right to make political decisions is instead exercised directly by citizens, acting under procedures of majority rule. The correct answer, therefore, is (A).

64. This question tests your knowledge of recent political behavior in European nations. Western European rightist political parties grew in strength and influence during the 1990's partly in reaction to the influx of foreign workers who were perceived as taking jobs from natives and threatening dominant cultures in host countries. The correct answer, therefore, is (D).

65. This question tests your knowledge of the parliamentary system. All pure parliamentary governments share a number of characteristics that may be contrasted with presidential or mixed systems of government. One of the distinguishing characteristics of a pure parliamentary system is the combination of the executive and legislative branches of government. The fact that the head of government must come from among the current members of the legislature is an example of the combination of branches, making (D) the correct answer.

GEOGRAPHY

66. This question asks you to identify a type of map used by geographers. A topographic map presents the horizontal and vertical positions of the landform's features through the use of relief marks that provide measurable elevation and other characteristics. The correct answer, therefore, is (B).

67. This question tests your ability to interpret a map and use your knowledge to identify significant connections. The maps above depict Earth's landmasses before the process of continental drift broke them apart. From these drawings, you can see that at one time the eastern coast of South America was joined with the western portion of Africa, and based on that, you should conclude that the two regions likely share certain geological features. The correct answer, therefore, is (A).

68. This question tests your knowledge of important geographic features of the world. Of the rivers listed as possible choices, the

Yangtze is in China, the Euphrates is located in the Middle East, and the Mekong is located in Southeast Asia, all parts of the Asian continent. The correct answer is (D), because the Nile is in Africa.

69. This question asks you to interpret a map of the world's time zones. According to the vertical divisions in the figure, you can see that Beijing is separated from Rio de Janeiro by eleven zones and that all of China keeps the same clock time, even though spread over five time zones. In order to calculate time, you should subtract an hour for each time zone as you travel from east to west, or add an hour for each zone as you travel from west to east. With this information, you can determine that if it is 9:00 A.M. on Wednesday in Beijing, it is eleven hours earlier—or 10:00 P.M. on Tuesday—in Rio de Janeiro. The correct answer, therefore, is (B).

70. This question tests two skills: your knowledge of basic geographical locations and your ability to read maps. Hong Kong is an island located in the South China Sea, off the southeastern coast of mainland China. You can determine Hong Kong's coordinates by calculating its latitude (the position north or south of the equator) and its longitude (the position east or west of the prime meridian). Hong Kong is approximately 20° north of the equator and 115° east of the prime meridian, and thus the correct answer is (A).

71. This question tests your basic knowledge of places, regions, and languages of the world. Of the pairs of cities listed above, only citizens of Lisbon and Rio de Janeiro share a common native language, which is Portuguese. The correct answer, therefore, is (B).

72. This question tests your ability to recognize important geographic locations. The Bosporus strait runs through the city of Istanbul, Turkey, and divides the continents of Europe and Asia. This prime location has long made Istanbul a major cultural and commercial center. The correct answer, therefore, is (D).

73. This question tests your knowledge of the rain forest biomes of the world. Although environmentalists became increasingly concerned during the 1990's as the Brazilian government extended transportation networks and resource development projects into the country's Amazon Basin, razing hundreds of thousands of acres of the region's lush tropical rain forest, the actual rate of deforestation as a percentage of the total area of rain forest has been moderate. About 5 percent of the total rain forest has been cleared. The rate of deforestation is highest in southern and southeastern Asia, primarily associated with commercial timber exploitation. The correct answer, therefore, is (C).

74. This question asks you to identify an important cause-and-effect relationship that determines climatic patterns in the United States. The jet stream is a high-velocity wind in the lower levels of the atmosphere that attains speeds of over 250 miles per hour as it moves in a westerly direction, carrying weather patterns with it. The correct answer, therefore, is (B).

75. This question asks you to make an inference from a map based on your knowledge of geography. Acid rain is precipitation that contains pollutants released into the atmosphere by the burning of fossil fuels.

As these contaminants become airborne, prevailing winds can carry them hundreds of miles, thus depositing them great distances from where they originated. The correct answer, therefore, is (A).

76. This question asks you to recall an important fact about the major religions of the world. The Middle East is the correct answer, (C).

77. This question tests your ability to interpret a set of graphs about global warming and to draw a conclusion from them. By combining the global warming potential created by the agricultural sectors of all three countries (represented by the darkly shaded portions of the columns) in each of the 20-year and 100-year projections, you can see that in both cases the energy sector of the United States alone still poses a greater threat for global warming. The correct answer, therefore, is (B).

78. This question tests your knowledge of water depletion in general and the Aral Sea in particular. In determining the answer, it is critical to keep in mind the fact that the Aral Sea contains freshwater, which has been diverted in great quantity by farmers hoping to grow cotton in the regions surrounding the lake. The correct answer, therefore, is (A).

79. This question asks you to use geography in order to interpret historical trends and events. Great Britain's geographical location between continental Europe and the New World allowed it to control trade networks during a period of rapid exploration and commercial expansion. The correct answer, therefore, is (A).

80. This question asks you to use your knowledge of world geography to answer a query about human societies. Because the political borders of many African countries do not correspond to those recognized by the continent's numerous tribal groups, many ethnic conflicts have erupted in sub-Saharan Africa, such as the 1994 Hutu massacre of the Tutsi minority in Rwanda. The correct answer, therefore, is (C).

ECONOMICS

81. This question tests your ability to associate an important economic principle with a specific case. Opportunity cost is the cost of the next best alternative use of money, time, or resources when one choice is made rather than another. The correct answer, therefore, is (D).

82. If the country specializes in producing the good in which it has a comparative advantage and engages in trade, it will get more units of Y for each unit of X than it was able to do before trade. That is, the country can import Y at a lower opportunity cost than it costs to produce it domestically. As a result, the country can consume combinations of goods X and Y that exceed its pretrade levels. The correct answer, therefore, is (A).

83. This question tests your knowledge of types of economic systems. Socialism is an economic system by which government decision-makers make decisions regarding the production and distribution of goods and services in key industries. The correct answer, therefore, is (A).

84. This question tests your knowledge of a definition of an important term. Monopoly is a market structure characterized by a single producer. The correct answer, therefore, is (D).

85. This question tests your knowledge of product markets generally and perfect competition specifically. Monopolies charge higher prices and produce less than competitors. The correct answer, therefore, is (A).

86. This question and the next one test your knowledge of the ways in which changes in supply and demand are related to price. A price ceiling that was repealed will cause the market to increase the price due to the previous shortage. As the price increases, the quantity supplied will increase and the quantity demanded will decrease. The correct answer, therefore, is (B).

87. At a price of P_3, the quantity demanded (Qd) will be at Q_1, and the quantity supplied (Qs) will be at (Q_3), or at a surplus, since Qs > Qd, the difference being Q_3-Q_1. The correct answer, therefore, is (C).

88. This question tests your knowledge of product markets. A characteristic of pure competition is that the firm produces a homogeneous product and is a small part of the total supply such that it cannot influence market price and total output. The correct answer, therefore, is (A).

89. This question tests your knowledge of factors markets. Resource markets include markets for the factors of production, including land, labor, and capital. (A), (C), and (D) are purchases made from product markets. The answer, therefore, is (B).

90. This question tests your knowledge of aggregate supply and aggregate demand models. A cycle of decreasing unemployment (or increasing employment) with an increase in consumption is characteristic of a recovery. The correct answer, therefore, is (C).

91. This question tests your ability to recognize an example of a general principle. A progressive tax is a tax for which the percentage of income paid in taxes rises as the level of income rises. The correct answer, therefore, is (B).

92. This question tests your ability to recognize the similarities between two important concepts. Declining economic activity during recession and depression results in high unemployment rates. The correct answer, therefore, is (B).

93. This question tests your knowledge of appropriate fiscal policies to deal with various economic states. During periods of increasing unemployment and declining gross domestic product (GDP), fiscal policy makers will attempt to stimulate the economy by pursuing policies of decreased taxation and increased government spending. Both increases in government spending and increases in consumption will help increase output and decrease unemployment. The correct answer, therefore, is (C).

94. This question tests your knowledge of appropriate monetary policy for dealing with inflation. When a country experiences inflation, the money supply should be restricted. This can be done by increasing the discount rate and selling bonds on the open market, both of which reduce the money supply. The correct answer, therefore, is (D).

95. This question tests your knowledge of the causes of economic growth. Economic growth is defined as an increase in the production possibility frontier. Growth can occur as the nation's productivity increases. The correct answer, therefore, is (A).

96. This question tests your knowledge of economic conditions and fiscal policies. Declining GDP and increasing unemployment rates would indicate the country is experiencing a recession. Appropriate fiscal policy would include decreasing personal income taxes to increase consumption and thereby increasing aggregate demand and GDP. The correct answer, therefore, is (A).

97. This question tests your ability to interpret a chart using only the information given. The graph indicates that from 1972 to 1987, the United States imported more consumer electronics than it exported. The correct answer, therefore, is (C).

98. This question tests your knowledge of cause and effect in basic economics. Trade deficit is the result of greater value of importation of goods and services relative to the value of exportation of goods and services. The correct answer, therefore, is (A).

99. This question tests your knowledge of international currency fluctuation. The value of the dollar in a flexible currency exchange system is partially dependent upon the demand for United States goods by foreign consumers. The correct answer, therefore, is (B).

100. This question tests your knowledge of why tariffs are used. Protective tariffs would restrict the variety of goods and services available. The correct answer, therefore, is (B).

101. This question tests your knowledge of a definition of an important term. Absolute advantage is a country's ability to produce more of a given product than another country can. The correct answer, therefore, is (A).

102. This question tests your knowledge of currency fluctuation. The United States dollar depreciated with respect to the British pound, since one dollar bought a smaller portion of a pound on March 1 compared to February 1. The dollar appreciated relative to the Japanese yen, since one dollar bought more yen on March 1 compared to February 1. The correct answer, therefore, is (C).

103. This question tests your knowledge of an important economic policy document. NAFTA was signed in 1993 to reduce tariffs between the United States, Canada, and Mexico. The correct answer, therefore, is (C).

BEHAVIORAL SCIENCES

104. This question asks you to recognize a major characteristic of the theories of an important psychologist. B. F. Skinner viewed human behavior in terms of physiological responses to the environment. He pioneered the study of operant conditioning in which behavior is either rewarded or punished. Skinner found that rewarding a behavior, which he called

positive reinforcement, led to an increase in the frequency of the behavior. The correct answer, therefore, is (B).

105. This question asks you to recognize the terminology and references in a quotation and assign them to a famous psychological theorist. Sigmund Freud believed that the human mind was composed of functional elements known as the ego, the id, and the superego. The id is composed of primitive desires for pleasure; the superego is composed of the internalization of social moral commands; the ego is the conscious mediator between an individual and reality. Since the quote refers to the relationship between the ego and the id, the correct answer is (D).

106. This question asks you to recognize an important social principle—socialization—and apply it to certain facts. Socialization is the process by which individual personality is formed through social influences. During the twentieth century, the influence of religion, the government, and voluntary associations on the average individual have generally waned. During this period, mass-communications media have grown considerably in size, power, and influence on individual personality development in the United States. The answer, therefore, is (A).

107. This question asks you to recognize an important principle of social organization—social mobility—and recognize an important condition for vertical social mobility. Social mobility involves the movement of individuals, families, or groups through a system of social hierarchy or stratification. Vertical mobility involves changes upward or

downward in position within the social classes. Of the four possible answers to the question, only income is a characteristic that is within the individual's power to change. All the other options are factors set at birth, and they thus limit social mobility. The correct answer, therefore, is (B).

108. This question asks you to recognize an important general social concept, the social institution. Social institutions are established organizations of positive significance to a society. They are usually dedicated to education, public service, or culture and preserve or propagate customs, practices, or relationships important to the community or society. Only answer (A), religion, meets these requirements.

109. This question asks you to recognize the effect of a certain important demographic trend in the United States in the pictured object. In the 1990's, Los Angeles, like many major American cities, received a large influx of immigrants of various cultural and ethnic backgrounds. The photograph shows a sign that carries Spanish- and Chinese-language advertisements. Because both Latino and Chinese populations are ethnic groups in the United States, the correct answer is (D).

110. This question asks you to recognize two important concepts concerning social justice and recognize the relationship between them. Prejudice is a bias or hostility toward members of a certain group; discrimination is the carrying out of that belief through deeds. Thus, prejudice is an attitude, and discrimination is an action. The correct answer, therefore, is (D).

111. This question asks you to recognize an important concept concerning social justice and recognize an example of it. Discrimination means carrying out prejudicial ideas through actual actions that exhibit bias and are unfair. Only the correct answer (B), a refusal, is an action rather than a state of mind.

112. This question asks you to recognize an important social event and identify a significant principle of social action—nonviolent protest. The 1963 March on Washington was a large gathering intended to peacefully protest racial discrimination and spur the government to take action. Although a crowd of such massive proportions could do much damage, the leaders of the movement insisted on the principle of nonviolent action, pioneered by the Indian leader Mahatma Gandhi, in order to highlight the justice of their cause. The correct answer, therefore, is (B).

113. This question asks you to recognize and understand a significant aspect of an important stage of human psychological development. One of the most serious challenges for an individual passing through adolescence is the development of a coherent, realistic sense of self. This sense of self must be integrated with accepted societal standards in order for the individual to function productively in society. The correct answer, therefore, is (C).

114. This question asks you to recognize an important issue in human personality development and psychological adjustment in the United States. While there are a number of different types of psychological disorders, the most common of the four choices listed above is depression, which according to a recent survey occurs in approximately 5 percent of the population of the United States. The correct answer, therefore, is (A).

115. This question asks you to interpret a chart using only the information it provides. The chart is organized with frequency of television viewing on the horizontal axis and the relative seriousness of criminal acts that are committed on the vertical axis. The chart reveals that as the frequency of television viewing increases, so does the seriousness of criminal acts committed. The graph therefore shows a positive correlation between the two, since an increase in one leads to an increase in the other. Causation is not addressed by the graph. The correct answer, therefore, is (D).

116. This question asks you to bring your knowledge of anthropology to a particular factual situation and apply important terms defining human cultural structure. A subculture is a group differentiated by ethnic, religious, or social factors that exhibits characteristic patterns of behavior that functionally unify the group and are sufficient to distinguish it from the surrounding culture or society. Both Hasidic Jews and Mennonites are relatively small religious groups with special social and cultural behaviors. The correct answer, therefore, is (B).

117. This question asks you to bring your knowledge of anthropology to a specific factual situation. Cultural diffusion is the spread of customs, beliefs, tools, and other aspects of a particular society to other groups of people over time. This can occur through trade, war, or simple contact. The correct answer, therefore, is (A).

Chapter 13
Are You Ready? Last-Minute Tips

▶ ▶ ▶ ▶ ▶ ▶ ▶ ▶ ▶ ▶ ▶ ▶

Checklist

Complete this checklist to determine if you're ready to take your test.

- ❏ Do you know the testing requirements for your teaching field in the state(s) where you plan to teach?

- ❏ Have you followed all of the test registration procedures?

- ❏ Do you know the topics that will be covered in each test you plan to take?

- ❏ Have you reviewed any textbooks, class notes, and course readings that relate to the topics covered?

- ❏ Do you know how long the test will take and the number of questions it contains? Have you considered how you will pace your work?

- ❏ Are you familiar with the test directions and the types of questions for your test?

- ❏ Are you familiar with the recommended test-taking strategies and tips?

- ❏ Have you practiced by working through the practice test questions at a pace similar to that of an actual test?

- ❏ If constructed-response questions are part of your test, do you understand the scoring criteria for these items?

- ❏ If you are repeating a Praxis Series Assessment, have you analyzed your previous score report to determine areas where additional study and test preparation could be useful?

The Day of the Test

You should have ended your review a day or two before the actual test date. And many clichés you may have heard about the day of the test are true. You should

- Be well rested

- Take photo identification with you

- Take a supply of well-sharpened #2 pencils (at least three)

- Eat before you take the test

- Be prepared to stand in line to check in or to wait while other test takers are being checked in

You can't control the testing situation, but you can control yourself. Stay calm. The supervisors are well trained and make every effort to provide uniform testing conditions, but don't let it bother you if the test doesn't start exactly on time. You will have the necessary amount of time once it does start.

You can think of preparing for this test as training for an athletic event. Once you've trained, and prepared, and rested, give it everything you've got. Good luck.

Appendix A
Study Plan Sheet

Study Plan Sheet

See Chapter 1 for suggestions on using this Study Plan Sheet.

STUDY PLAN						
Content covered on test	How well do I know the content?	What material do I have for studying this content?	What material do I need for studying this content?	Where could I find the materials I need?	Dates planned for study of content	Dates completed

Appendix B

For More Information

► ► ► ► ► ► ► ► ► ► ► ►

Educational Testing Service offers additional information to assist you in preparing for the Praxis Series™ Assessments. *Tests at a Glance* booklets and the *Registration Bulletin* are both available without charge (see below to order). You can also obtain more information from our Web site: www.ets.org/praxis/.

General Inquiries

Phone: 609-771-7395 (Monday-Friday, 8:00 A.M. to 7:45 P.M., Eastern time)
Fax: 609-771-7906

Extended Time

If you have a learning disability or if English is not your primary language, you can apply to be given more time to take your test. The *Registration Bulletin* tells you how you can qualify for extended time.

Disability Services

Phone: 609-771-7780
Fax: 609-771-7906
TTY (for deaf or hard-of-hearing callers): 609-771-7714

Mailing Address

Teaching and Learning Division
Educational Testing Service
P.O. Box 6051
Princeton, NJ 08541-6051

Overnight Delivery Address

Teaching and Learning Division
Educational Testing Service
Distribution Center
225 Phillips Blvd.
P.O. Box 77435
Ewing, NJ 08628-7435

NOTES: